Kathleen
May He continue
to walk this home school
journey with you
Mari Fitz-Wynn

Take Heart

26 Steps to a Healthy Home School

Mari Fitz-Wynn

Take Heart - 26 Steps to a Healthy Home School
Mari Fitz-Wynn
www.heartforhomeschool.org
heartforhomeschoolministries@gmail.com

Published 2014, by Light Messages
www.lightmessages.com
Durham, NC 27713
Printed in the United States of America
ISBN: 978-1-61153-106-0

Contents

Take Heart i
Dedication v
Acknowledgments vi
Introduction 1
Anxiety and Anticipation 5
Burnout 10
Character 16
Disillusion 19
Expectations 22
First Day of School 26
Goals 28
Home School 32
Inspiration 38
Juggle 41
Kids 43
Legacy 47
Mastery 51
No 55

Organized.....59
Pitfalls.....63
Quitting.....66
Random.....69
Support Groups.....76
Testing.....81
Unit Studies.....84
Volunteer.....88
X.....95
Yes.....97
Zowie.....99
Conclusion.....101
Questions.....105

Dedication

This book is dedicated to every mom who had the seed of home education planted in her heart and watched it grow into a reality.

Special thanks to Pam Bynem, Chris Sexton, Julie Starrett, and Donna Taylor—who helped to water my seed.

Acknowledgments

No one writes a book alone. I am so grateful to God for giving me the idea to write a book, the energy I needed to research and the tenacity to continue writing when life became difficult.

I also want to thank my family who gave me the rich experiences that helped shape each topic in this book. No student, no home school, and without either there would be no book today.

A special thanks to my daughter Rooney who helped me with the typing when I feared I'd fall asleep at the computer and wake up to indecipherable gibberish. Special thanks to Keifer Wynn and Donna Aguilar for proof reading each draft of this book.

I also want to extend a great deal of gratitude to my close friend and mentor Dixie McClintock who untiringly edited this book, Kadi Kool and Bria Arline for helping to proofread, and also to Scott McClintock for his technical assistance.

God bless each of you.

Dear Reader,

Thank you for purchasing this book. I hope you are blessed as you join me in remembering our home school journey.

It's impossible to put the experiences of a 18-year journey into a few words; however this is a book of lessons I've learned and would like to share with you. These are lessons I discovered helped, healed or held steady our home school experience from start to finish.

Is your home school limping along, scattered or chaotic? Is the temperature in the classroom feverish and the pulse for learning weakening by the day? Is your school new and struggling to survive? Is there any hope for your home school?

Take heart, the doctor is in and ready to help yours become a healthier, happier home school.

Mari

Introduction

There was a mom
Who held a job
That took her from
The home she loved

Each day there was
a stifled cry
She kissed each child
and waved good bye

For off to school
They all did go
Lunches and books
Markers in tow

Six long hours
They were away
From this dear mom
Most every day

First of all, I need to tell you that there has always been the tug in my heart to spend time with my children. That grew grew and wrapped itself around my heart as a vise when, as a working mom, I had to return to work after the cursory three months maternity leave. The vice grew tighter, as I began to make strides in my professional career, leaving home and family to travel across the state and country. Yet, no matter how much I accomplished, the "tug" would still be there. While taking little ones to childcare; "tug" when dropping older ones off at school; "tug" as a professional career woman and mother. I soon discovered that weekends were never long enough. The end-of-school breaks and vacations became tortuous. There was never enough time together nor was there any escaping the "tugs."

I should also tell you that I stumbled upon the philosophy of home education, as it were, by some divine foot stuck out to trip or, at least, slow me down. Professionally, I was on the fast track for management, and had learned quite well how to ignore the "tug" when necessary.

But one day, while rummaging through a recycled magazine bin, my eyes fell upon a magazine that immediately caught my attention. On the cover was a wonderful photo of a happy and smiling family dressed in matching outfits. That's right, everyone was smiling, and yet there seemed to be more than the smile speaking to me. That special thing was contentment. Yes, that was it. I glanced at the name of the magazine, and there it was again, the "tug." Placing all the other magazines back into the bin, I walked off with my sole treasure of the day.

I realize now the "tug" I felt was the Holy Spirit gently drawing me to another level of motherhood. That was 18 years ago. I had discovered a concept that would allow me an opportunity to spend quality, quantity and even quiet time with my family. This idea would support both my husband's and my desire to provide a solid Christian education for our children without the high cost of a private Christian school. We would have control over the direction of their learning and confidence in the classes specifically tailored to their interests and learning styles. What's more, we could plan vacations and spontaneous family getaways as we desired rather than be bound to several different class calendars and school activities.

That treasured magazine served as my introduction to home schooling and gave me the immediate conviction that home education was a viable option for our family. I read that magazine from cover to cover three times. I could hardly wait for my husband to return home from work, so excited was I to share this discovery with him. With the children in bed and the end of the evening ours, I happily read the magazine again, this time with my husband. Feeling quite like the home school expert, I pointed out articles and specific segments that I felt were of great significance or particular interest. How relieved I was to find that he shared my excitement and enthusiasm. We agreed that we did not need to pray about whether or not this was the right decision for our family. We definitely would home school our children. We just needed to pray about when we would get started.

My initial reaction to the idea of home education? It sounded wonderful, almost too good to be true. Yet the benefits I have just mentioned are but a few of the many blessings and benefits our family has derived from the decision to home school. The weekends took on a completely different meaning after I began teaching at home. We no longer had to race through the weekend in order to complete a long list of plans and activities, while household chores stared menacingly around each corner. I didn't have to feel guilty over having to choose between spending our time together having fun or doing chores.

Our school schedule fluctuated from year to year and I enjoyed the freedom to decide which days we would have math or science, and how long we would study.

I am as excited about home education today as I was so many years ago.

If you are thinking about home education, let me share some thoughts with you that have helped me to keep a fresh perspective about home schooling over the years:

- Pray, and pray again, and again, until you are ready to lay aside your plans for His.
- Make your commitment. Sometimes this requires limiting and surrendering personal and some family pursuits.
- Clarify your objectives. The decision to home school may have started from an emotional standpoint, but soon you will find, as I did that, the reality of everyday teaching responsibilities will eventually kick in. Know why you want to teach your children and what you want to teach them.
- Acknowledge your limitations, but ignore the self doubt and feelings of incompetence that inevitably arise.
- Determine from the start that home school is and will be more than just a meaningful educational experience for your children. Let it become a lifestyle for your whole family.
- Remember, school, curriculum, plans and the student are ultimately in God's control. This releases us. Relax and take things one day, one lesson, one subject and one problem at a time.

Expect trials and errors in finding the best road for you and your family to travel.

Expect an adventure!

Anxiety and Anticipation

Anxiety and anticipation were two emotions that seemed to dominate most of the space in my heart and mind. Since I decided to say "yes" to the conviction which seemed so strongly placed upon my heart to teach my children at home, I was excited but anxious.

The anxiety was there simply because it was a first step in completely unchartered territory for anyone in my large family of seven siblings, numerous cousins, aunts and uncles. I was also anxious about providing the best opportunities for learning life skills, academics, and social development.

Here is a list of a few of the statements we wrote out to help quash our anxieties and remind us of the benefits our children would derive from home schooling:

- Provide a warm and nurturing environment that would build their self esteem and self confidence:
- Provide materials and field trips to keep them excited about learning.
- Keep them firmly on their spiritual path as they grew into maturity.

- Prepare them to pursue academic excellence after graduation from home school.

So while that all sounded wonderful on paper, I didn't know then that I didn't have a clue about how to make it happen. The more I read and researched, the easier it sounded. I started on my merry way into the world of home education, thinking I just might be miles ahead of the other "newbies," as they were referred to, because I read a few "how to" home school books and articles.

Some of the books also referred to home school moms who had taught more than five years as "veteran home educators." I remember reading one article in particular where the mom said she was so clueless that it took her a couple of years before she realized she was actually moving in the wrong direction. Again, in my well-researched and studied ways, I thought I had a clue. Besides, I didn't know anyone who was a veteran. As a matter of fact, I didn't know a single family that was home schooling. Failing to connect or meet a "vet" or mentor to help me out, I also figured, how hard can it be?

Was I ever wrong, but I didn't know it yet!

Although I had unofficially started home schooling my children during what was to be their last year in traditional school, my idea to start home school was a plan similar to the one given to Noah: I would bring my children home from traditional school, two by two. (The toddler didn't count in that number, as he was already at home, and I would start him when the second youngest was ready to begin.)

I was batting 1000 and was quite pleased with my plan. I proceeded to withdraw the first two from school. When my first two weeks of school ended, so did my perfect home school growth and development plan. Hurricane Fran arrived, and turned out to be one of the most destructive hurricanes to hit North Carolina. In the wake of the catastrophic storm, all schools in the area were shut down.

So there I was attempting to teach the two original or experimental home school students, with the others in the background wondering why they couldn't be home schooled, too! After a few days of listening to their lament, and the news that schools in our county would not open for a very long time, I decided to bite the bullet and just bring the others into home schooling at once. It was still September, so I figured I had plenty of time to start school all over, again, because I didn't know I was clueless.

After a year and a half, I soon came to realize my foot had been on the gas pedal and I had been driving into the metaphorical brick wall for all that time. I was suddenly struck with a "new revelation," that I didn't really have much of a clue about what I was doing. As I crashed into that brick wall, I wondered why I had thought I could actually teach my children at home. So I spent the remainder of the year asking questions like crazy from anyone and everyone I could possibly think to ask questions of, beginning with "Do you know anyone who home schools?"

(Please read the following chapters on "Burnout" and Support Groups to learn how I resolved this issue.)

Right now, I want to discuss the impact of anxiety on my ability to teach during the first year and a half. Things were running remarkably smoothly throughout the first couple of months that first year. But then the following began to happen and anxiety set in big time:

- I began to notice how difficult it was for me to stick with the schedule for classes. I literally had more classes and students than I did daylight hours.
- My workload was immediately more than doubled, now that I had brought the rest of the children home, not to mention a toddler underfoot.

- I also had to deal with all of the administrative tasks such as grading papers, making assignments, and grading those assignments.
- Academics are the foundation of home education, no argument here. There is absolutely no getting around the fact that eventually our children need to learn to read, write, add and subtract, etc., in order to function in society. You will accomplish this goal. However, if you worry that you will not provide the "wonderful, high quality" education that is supposed to be the end result of the whole home school experience, you are in good company. But let that be the end of your worry. A healthy dose of understanding that we should not rely completely on ourselves and our ability helps on the days when it's tough and you are feeling anxious and over whelmed.

Go to the One who desires to take all of our worries and cares. Take a break and focus on the love and personal attention you are able to shower on your student. Otherwise, over-anxiety will turn to panic, panic to discouragement, and discouragement to giving up the home school experience completely. You'll end up putting your children on the first yellow school bus you see.

I was once an anxiety-ridden home school mom. People would often ask me, "What are you doing?" and in truth I would frequently ask myself the same question. As I prayed, the anxiety ceased and the anticipation started to abound, not only in me, but in the children as well.

After several years of teaching experience, I came to the conclusion that no one is always 100% confident of what they're doing when it comes to home education. My many friends who home school often swing on a pendulum that shows a high level of confidence; but then, all it takes is one seemingly simple question answered incorrectly by their student, and the pendulum swings the other way: "I'm a failure; I'm ruining my child's chance at a quality education."

Just remember: the task set before you is not easy, nor is it impossible. This task is God-given, and with that knowledge in mind, start counting down the days until your home school starts up again. While the early years of our home school were probably the most emotionally, physically, and spiritually challenging time of my life, they presented some remarkably eye-opening teaching opportunities, as well as learning opportunities, for me as a mom and teacher.

> Remember, the task set before you is neither too easy nor is it impossible!

Burnout

Please find me a stick, a scissor, and sheet;
My schedule and goals I no longer can meet
Worksheets, assignments, and tests are piled high
Get out of bed early for class? I don't try!
I'm tired and weary, I no longer feel brave,
Just let me my flag of surrender now wave.

What happens when a creative, enthusiastic home educator finds that the wonderful activities, projects and learning well has suddenly run dry? What happens when lunch dates and shopping dates with "the girls" have more appeal than history dates? It's called "burnout," the one small glitch in this otherwise wonderful endeavor called home school.

I remember the very first time I entered a period of burnout. After one year of intense disciplined teaching, writing my own unit studies, planning all the appropriate field trips, creating and administering each student's quizzes and exams, I found myself dreading another day of school, another lesson, another plan…another student.

Amazingly, I, the dedicated teacher, had become easily distracted, and was avoiding all educational pursuits like the plague. As daily work assignments began to stack up into mountains of paper, and we increased our P.E. days, I also had several Teacher Work Days in a row *(days in which the teacher sadly did not work).*

Daily, I felt more and more overwhelmed with what I needed to do and accomplish, versus what I actually felt like doing. My motivation to teach was dying a slow death.

For all my time spent researching the home school option, burnout and the dwindling of motivation had not been covered, or even mentioned. Where had I fallen short? What was wrong with me? We would certainly not have any photo ops for the cover of any home school magazine now.

Years later, looking back down that road, I realize experiencing burnout is a common season in the lives of most teachers; home, public and private. Burnout is sometimes a result of "how" we home school, but more often than not, it is the culmination of many factors. There are a few warning signals to alert us of its encroachment. Here are a few of the lessons I've learned:

1. **Stop School** - No, I don't mean confetti-in-the-air-and-cheers-all-around stopping of school. Just give yourself and your students a break. Whether one day or two, as you feel yourself burning out, an intermission is certainly warranted and well deserved. When you feel as though the walls are beginning to close in on you, or tensions start to run high, a teacher work day is probably in order. This time off will allow mom an opportunity to regroup, re-organize, and revive that love of teaching. This is the ideal time to pray for your school and teaching endurance. It will definitely give you a fresh start for the next day.

1. One friend gave me this advice from her own experience with burnout. "Give yourself permission to take the day off and be together. Go to the park, do something that includes everyone, or alter your school plans to include lots of independent work for the children. Take this time to remind yourself and your children how much you really love and enjoy each other.
2. **Find support** - Initially, I believed that home school support groups were a fine idea for those that needed them. First of all, I reasoned we had enough children to strike down the socialization argument. Secondly, I planned all of our field trips. Besides, I wanted field trips that were perfectly coordinated with our studies, and often the "planned" support group field trips were not. (Don't ask me how I knew this.) Thirdly, I was just too busy teaching my children to be involved in something like a support group. What I did not realize then was that each of my reasons for not joining a group was based solely on the needs I perceived I was already meeting for the children. I had left myself entirely out of the equation and now I was the one burning out. With this new revelation, you may ask, how long did it take me to remedy the situation? I immediately found a white pillowcase, tied it to a stick, waved it and started looking for a support group.
3. **Get Help** - As a new home school mom, I believed that I had to do it all; teaching, grading, project building, transporting etc. Since my husband was a full time pastor and worked part time out of the home, I felt it my "duty" to let him rest when he came in and so I did not involve him to any extent with the day-to-day teaching activities. Big mistake! I was burning myself out by not utilizing my greatest and most obvious source of help - my spouse.

He enjoyed math; I hated it! Yet I continued to teach and grade papers on a subject that I loathed. The light came on one day as I, almost completely discouraged and quite weary of silently bearing my burden, finally decided to express to my husband how much I dreaded looking at another math paper (I figure there was a little bit of pride mixed in there as well) I'm not certain as to why I had pictured myself as being able to teach it all. The words "Let me do it," never sounded sweeter. Trust me, it seemed as if the birds outside struck up a chorus while dogs and cats in the neighborhood barked and meowed in harmony. The dark cloud over our home school parted and beams of sunshine poured in.

4. **Change Your Routine** - On the one hand, routine is necessary. Establishing a routine for your family works well when the students are very young. They will know what to expect on Mondays or Thursday for example. However, more of the same every day leads to what? Burnout! Change is great and sometimes it's all we need to give our students and school a "pick me up!" It didn't take long for me to learn that our children did not want to sit for long periods of time to "do school." Behaviors that I interpreted as disinterest with the subject or some pronouncement on my teaching ability were merely the early symptoms of burnout, (in most instances).

That home school students could burnout was a revelation; that ***my*** students were burning out was startling! I quickly instituted "special days," times when we broke our daily school routine.

Here are a few fun suggestions that worked really well for us. Some have become official school day traditions:

- **Backwards Day** - Everyone *(even the teacher)* wears their clothing backwards, and the school schedule is observed in reverse.
- **Pajama Day** - self-explanatory. *(I shared this idea with a friend, she stared at me blankly. Her comment was this: "Our special day is actually getting dressed to do school!" Okay, never mind!)*
- **Color Day** - No school colors? Here's a great way to reinforce family and school unity: come up with some.
- **Bored Day** - Aha! Fooled you, didn't I? This is when we spend most of the day playing board games related to our unit study, topic or class subject *(e.g. science, math, geography, etc.)*
- **Opera Day** - Gifted or not, everything is sung operatically for the entire school day
- **Day of Silence** - Communication is only by ASL. *(Our students learned ASL-American Sign Language as their foreign/second language.)*
- **Heroes and Heroines Day** - Our students dressed as their favorite historical figure. We usually videotaped this

5. **Pray** - Add prayer to your "to do list." Whether first thing in the morning, last thing at night or during the middle of the day, a quiet time with the Lord is a must. His direction is not given simply because we need it. It is given because we ask. I learned to find out from the Father how He wanted to order my day, and prayed earnestly that I would follow those orders!
6. I had been overwhelmed to the point that I wanted to walk away. I longed to enjoy teaching again. Then, with the help of my spouse, I would make progress. Later in life, as a widowed single mom, it was important for me to connect with other single moms and barter, as

it were, for services, classes or help on special projects. In other words, sometimes our friends become our greatest resources when we find ourselves without the help of a husband at home.

Watch for the warning signals of burnout.

Character

Whatever academic goals you set for your students should be accompanied and complemented by character goals drawn from the principles of godly childrearing found in the Bible. As parents, we want to instruct our children to be respectful, kind, considerate, honest, and trustworthy. Hundreds of academic accolades cannot outweigh the value of teaching moral integrity to our children. The importance of setting and upholding standards of excellence cannot be overstated. We aimed our teaching to reach the heart, impress the spirit, and develop a philosophy that formed a framework for establishing character goals early in the lives of our children.

Initiating character goals early for your child is very important, and experience has proven that our academic goals accompanied by character goals produce end results, which will make you proud of your children.

I cannot begin to count the number of hours I have spent on the phone with moms, counseling, consoling and comforting, because of the heartbreak they were experiencing due to a child who sassed back continuously, cheated on school work and tests, or lied constantly. My advice is always the same.

Stop teaching and deal with the character issues. There is never any learning taking place in that type of setting.

There are three primary areas of character development we identified and used to teach our children. The philosophy is basically that of instructing heart and spirit. Character traits have to be consistently cultivated. Let me share three that I feel are most important:

- **Possessing an excellent spirit** - Self-control, consideration of others, and submission to authority are all attributes of a child with an excellent spirit. An "excellent" spirit does not mean that the child is always excellent or perfect. It simply means that the child accepts instruction, challenges, and correction without displays of temper or tantrums. Children may not always listen or even appreciate our instruction or suggestions, especially as they grow older. However, as we have lovingly invested our time to train them to maintain an excellent spirit, eventually they will understand that instruction and correction are given only when needed. Without correction, the child's academic and spiritual path will be unclear for them.
- **Respectful Attitude** - Transmit your respectful attitude to your children. I'd like to encourage you to be careful in this area. Many times we send a message to our children that contradicts our testimony. Children need to see their parents giving and receiving respect from one another at home, and showing respect to the children as well. A careless remark about someone's appearance, speech, or even their opinion may give your children a wrong message. It may sometimes be challenging. However, I think it most wonderful for children to see our teaching validated by the way we live. It actually serves another purpose. Their thoughts are strengthened, not damaged, by what they perceive

(and are shown) about our level of belief or seriousness about what we've been teaching.

- **Willing Obedience** - I read an article once, where the author stressed the point that obedience to parents, because of a child's inner conviction, is truly an honor to God. What a worthy goal to make our own! During the younger years, it is relatively easy to develop an outward show of obedience or conformity in your child. However, as they grow up and become mature and more independent, your child will begin to understand that submission to authority pleases God, which will also produce a teachable spirit in your student. During their preteen and teen years, there is a greater need for the student to learn self-discipline, which works hand in hand with obedience.

Teach your child to listen to you and to obey you at home and away from home. (This can be reinforced through games, like Simon Says and Mother, May I?) Remind them that this is also honoring to God. This training will help years down the road when mom or dad may not be physically present to help them with tough decisions or in the challenging moments away from home. I believe that my children will have the necessary tools (teaching) to make their decisions based on a true and deep conviction of wanting to be obedient to God's Word.

Deal with character issues immediately and lovingly!

Disillusion

"Oh Mother Dear," the children cried,
As they sat down right by my side
"Please tell again, though late at night
How much we love to read and write
We share so well, we never fight
Happy children, as you can see
Joy and delight, you must agree!"

There was that brief moment in the very beginning of our home school, once upon a time, where I daydreamed and fantasized of such moments and conversations with my "dear, sweet children."

Our days would be spent cuddled beside one another on the sofa, in front of a roaring fire with a faithful dog resting at our feet. Now and then I would pause and gaze lovingly at my children, blowing them kisses for rising early enough to complete their household chores, eat breakfast, have devotions, and begin school on time, without having to be told or reminded. Why, in that wonderful home school dream, my children did indeed love to learn about everything all the time. There were also great crowds of loving, supportive neighbors who only wanted a glimpse into our backyard to see the children's most recent projects, such as a replica of the Mayflower and a small-scale Egyptian pyramid.

However, as time wore on, I found out that reading, writing, and actually loving it were not everyday occurrences in our school. I am pleased to admit our children were very well behaved and did not fight; they got along well, for the most part. Yet when they disagreed, it was a major disagreement! Oh, the stories I could tell about character development, unmet goals, incomplete school work, and my staring enviously as the yellow school bus rolled down the street.

Let's get away from our sweet tale and my fantasy about teaching the children. When I realized that I was chasing a "happily ever after," which, in fact, could never ever be my reality, I really began to understand the purpose of home education. This was not a concept or theory to be studied and read about, but a lifestyle to be lived and enjoyed. I understood that the word "perfecting," not "perfect," would often apply to our home school family, although it took me a while. The idea of a trophy home, marriage, children, and trophy school was not only unrealistic, it was unattainable. It certainly was not a goal the Father would allow or make possible for me to achieve.

I eventually learned that there is no magic curriculum that adjusts itself to each student and no ideal days for learning math. Unfortunately the older children became the experiments by which I gained this knowledge. Most importantly, I learned that the school, students, and teacher truly belong to a loving Father. He wanted me to embrace His ways and His direction for our school.

In order to do that, I needed to be aware of the task I had undertaken and the limitations I would face if I chose to home school in my own strength and ability. Some days I was utterly disillusioned with the results. I will never forget His gentle whisper of encouragement to assure a happy ending: "teach, learn and live in the here and now" by His daily direction. I found out that trusting in His plan takes the pressure off us. Following His plan means accepting His results and we no longer have to feel guilty or defeated if our students don't measure up to the children of our fellow home school friends. What a relief to know that His definition of success is different for each family, student and school!

From where you sit, you may not consider any of our accomplishments successful. Happily, I've learned not to burden myself down with outside opinions. What I also learned was to follow His instruction and direction which made it easier to teach my children how to follow mine. Then, as now, I recognized that sometimes, in spite of an abundance of the best curriculum, sound biblical teaching, and our best efforts as parents, wrong choices and decisions are made. Perhaps there were road signs along the way that we missed, or holes in the fences we didn't realize needed to be mended, but our story is written by the Master Author.

Though we may veer from time to time away from His perfect plan for our school and miss a few of the perfectly scripted lines He's written for us, He is faithful and promises to bring the happy ending to pass, which for us, was graduation day.

In spite of our best efforts,
we will make mistakes,
as will our children.

Pushing through the hard times
is the key
to successful home schooling!

Expectations

What does your child expect from home school? What benefits will your child ascribe to being educated at home? Take time to think about that and then ask your child, "What do you expect from home school?"

Based on the child's level of maturity and whether the home school is just starting, ask another question as directly as you are able: "How do you like home school?" or "Why do you like home school?" It's possible that some of their answers might surprise, shock, and even catch you off guard! Don't let the fear of the answers cause you not to ask such a question. It is amazing the thoughts that will emerge from our children when we slow down enough to listen.

Many times we are focused on making certain that our children meet our expectations with assignments, progress, test taking, learning, etc. We have found that there is a clear advantage to talking with our children and discussing their thoughts regarding home schooling. Don't you find that you always learn something from a conversation with your children? Hopefully your child is comfortable enough to voice an opinion about why home education is important and, as the child matures, to explain why and how much home education has benefited him.

As long as a child understands that you really are interested, that the answers to the questions will not jeopardize future discussions in any way, and that there is no "right" or "wrong" answer, the child should feel free to speak up and share his feelings about what's good or bad about home school. He must have the assurance of knowing that if he expresses his honest opinion regarding the things about home school that he might like to change or do differently, he may do so without repercussions.

While I am not advocating that the child dictate to the parent what is to be learned or studied, or how often classes should be scheduled, it is important that the child know how much you value his input and that his opinions about home schooling are very important. Otherwise, the educational direction begins to look like the mass education process from which we may have removed or deliberately protected them.

One blessing of frank discussions with our children has been to identify problems or issues that might not have otherwise come up. Unless you specifically ask your child if he feels home schooling is meeting his expectations, issues that have not been discussed or unidentified may sometimes cause a child to "act out" or present certain inappropriate behaviors born out of frustration, anger or boredom.

Very often the child's idea of home schooling is not the same as the one the parents have. This is one reason why it is a good idea to have your school's vision and goals written out and posted for all to see, or written down in their notebooks. I have a friend that laminates their school's vision and makes it part of the child's notebook cover.

Once we are aware of the child's expectations, there may exist some areas in which we as the parent/teacher are able to adapt, revise, and rethink our approach to teaching, topics and tasks. This allows us the opportunity to align our students' expectations with our own, both of which will hopefully produce a satisfactory learning environment.

One final advantage to consider is that you are able to plan for courses of study, direct or guided study, borrow or purchase any curriculum and supplemental learning tools based on the child's input.

Our children do need to know and understand the clear lines of parental authority and understand that there are certain elements within the home school that are not open for discussion or that are not likely to change simply because the children think they should.

Not all children will immediately see or reap the benefits of a home education; so be patient. On the other hand, there are families that are not as successful with home schooling as they had desired to be, and for them, a peaceful home exists when some or all of the children return to school outside the home.

How do we encourage our children to take an active part in the planning of special projects, field trips, and so forth? Encouragement comes by allowing them the opportunity to help with the planning of a few of the classes they will take the coming year and by finding out which of the current curricula excites their interests or seems to be the most informative. Which books are boring or hard to understand? Some parents give their children the opportunity to attend book fairs and curriculum shares to see firsthand what a certain curriculum looks like and is all about. I like to pass on the various curriculum and book catalogs to my students. They will usually look through them several times and then begin to mark off items as "highly interesting," "looks interesting," and "no, thanks." I have found this to be invaluable when making purchases.

Allowing this type of input from our children not only encourages them, but us as well, and helps our quest for finding interesting and effective curricula for them. Believe me, it is well worth the time and effort to encourage this type of input from your children and, in the long run, it produces great expectations for the new school year.

While talking with your student from the beginning about why you have chosen to home school, find out about their expectations for school at home!

First Day of School

I am not a huge proponent of home school mimicking public or private school. However, if there is a tried and true idea that works at home that originated in a public or private school arena, I say, run with it.

In public and private schools, the first and last days of school are generally filled with excitement, and I adopted this same philosophy for our school. Early on, I endeavored to make our first day of school unforgettable, one that the students would look forward to with much enthusiasm.

I believe I succeeded when we started our third year and our students began asking in July what we'd be doing for the first day of school in August! It was also at that point I decided they needed to take ownership of at least part of that day's events. I started asking them, beginning with the oldest, to give us suggestions and help us plan activities. It was such a joy to see how thrilled they became, as they were included in decisions.

Here's a list of our first day of school activities (for many of which we invited one or two other home school families to join us):

1. Have a picnic with old-fashioned field day games.
2. Decorate the schoolroom with posters and streamers.
3. Scan family photos onto banner size paper and make a "Welcome Back to School" banner.
4. Do you have school colors? The first three days of school we dressed in our school colors to celebrate school unity.
5. Plan and take a field trip that kicks off your first unit or major area of study.
6. Have a family concert.
7. Celebrate staying up late one last weekend by having a special movie festival.
8. Do something unexpected. One year we all dyed our hair blue (spray on, wash off).
9. Fix a special breakfast the weekend before school starts.
10. Enjoy a backyard barbecue.

Celebrate the start
of a brand new school year
and forget about the difficult
end to last year's school.

Create momentum
for starting school
by planning a special day.

Goals

It is my thought that every home school should have a vision and goals. Goals, no matter how loosely formed, are an important part of home school functionality. In the beginning, you might consider your goals to be the same as your expectations, which is great. Throughout your child's education and the growth of your school, these expectations will begin to take shape through the achievement of goals. In essence, the responsibility of setting goals for your student is ongoing.

While this is not to say that everything must be written down and planned out, but certainly, the framework for what you hope to accomplish during the year should be fleshed out from time to time. Moreover, it will be difficult to achieve the vision of where you'd like to be by year's end, let alone the end of the day, if you can't articulate your vision on paper. Writing down our vision keeps us accountable to our students (and ourselves) and will hopefully help us to stay on track.

Whether you are the type of person that likes flexibility and spontaneity, or you have the type of personality that works well within a very structured environment, the overall vision for your home school must be in your heart and mind in order for it to become a reality.

I believe there are basically three steps to writing goals:

1. A plan of action
2. Clearly stated goals
3. Realistic objectives

Plan of action

This is simply a statement or plan of what you intend to do. If you've pulled a child out of a traditional school setting and the child struggled with math and reading, your plan of action would include methods by which you hope to bring the child up to current grade level in those subjects.

How you intend to do that would be the other part of your action plan, e.g. using supplemental learning tools via computer, flash cards etc., or utilizing the services of a tutor or on-line program.

Another element of the action plan would be to determine the education path for your child. In other words, how many grades do you intend for your child to complete?

Clearly stated goals

Once you've determined that you will teach your child from K-6th, 8th, or 12th, you will be able to put your goals down on paper.

Some families choose to use their state's Standards of Education in which case it is easier to identify your standards relative to your academic goals. Once you've identified what you would like to see as the end result, begin to write short term goals. The short term goals are part of the process you will need to follow in order to accomplish the long-term goals.

During the early days of our home school, a friend of mine but not of *home schooling*, suggested that I not set such high and lofty goals for my children, as she was aware that a few of them had learning disabilities. Needless to say, I was much taken aback by her suggestion.

Rather than set the standard for learning to their disability, we kept the potential to excel academically within reach of each child. We set goals and objectives we felt were achievable, but not overwhelming. Remember the objectives need to be realistic, regardless of the child's academic giftedness.

Realistic objectives

Set the standards high for your student with no apologies and no compromises. Don't look the other way if your child attempts to cheat, take short cuts, or use any other dishonest methods to accomplish the academic goals you've given him. Mediocrity remains the order of the day in so many educational institutions. Pushing our students to excel to their full learning ability alleviates that mindset.

- High academic standards do not equate to straight A's and a staggeringly high grade point average. There should not be pressure on the student get a perfect score. Instead, encourage your student to work to his fullest potential.
- Do not discourage your child by setting goals that are out of his ability or capability to attain.
- Remind your child that the objectives are there to serve as a guide and reminder of what you expect them to accomplish, not as a flag of failure or defeat.
- Keep the objectives realistic and try not to be overly optimistic about what can be accomplished during a single school year.
- As your child accomplishes many of his own goals, celebrate them. This will enhance the learning process and help him/her to see the bigger picture of where

you are directing him/her with the home school objective.

- Revisit the goals with your students periodically so that the children are reminded that what they are doing has value and is moving them forward toward accomplishing this phase of their education.

Remember: Know where to aim your school arrow by developing a clearly stated vision and goals.

Home School

There are as many ideas about home schooling as there are approaches to home education. Some families feel "led" to home educate. Others feel "called." Some families determine home school for them is grades K-12. Still others only want to teach through middle school, saving attending high school outside the home as a special experience.

What significance do you place upon the words "home school?" Individual family preferences help to define that significance. Our goals and vision for our children are also defined by it. So, how do you spell "home school?" Here are some thoughts to contemplate:

H = Honor. Do you count it an honor to teach your children? Do you believe it to be an honor to have primary responsibility for their education? The privileges, blessings and tough times give us a clearer picture of God's Hand in all we attempt to do. That He would give us opportunity to educate "His" children is indeed an honor. Do not take it lightly.

Or would you say "H" stands for "hard?" We all have those "I just can't do it" days. The key to surviving, no, succeeding, lies in maintaining focus and honoring the commitment to teach our children.

O = Obedience. Is obedience displayed in your home: children to parents, parents to the Lord and His Word? Without biblically defined obedience, there can truly be little or no obedience. A home, let alone a schoolroom, full of disobedient children equals a quick and easy formula for disaster. Children that won't obey won't learn.

For some, **"O" may mean "obstacle."** Is your day full of seemingly insurmountable problems and interruptions? A ringing telephone, drop-by friends, stacks of papers waiting for grades? Learn to distinguish between circumstances, concerns and obstacles that get in the way of your school day; and other situations or interruptions that cause an unnecessary break from your daily routine.

M = Motivated. It's my goal to start and end each school day as a motivated teacher! There have been days when this goal was not realized. My children didn't always inspire me to teach, and I'm sure I don't always inspire them to learn. I've learned to recognize the early warning signs of losing motivation, such as my desire to run the opposite way from my approaching students! This I have come to learn is a clear indication of my dwindling motivation. It is also an indication that I'm veering too far into my plans and farther away from God's. Knowing what to do, prayerfully seeking and then following His plan, keeps me refreshed and renewed. It automatically spills over to my lesson plans and teaching. This makes it easier to pass on that same motivation to my children.

What if the **"M" here means "mundane"** to you? Perhaps your school curriculum, environment, or schedule could use a face-lift. Take time to evaluate each aspect of your home school. Looking at the same unchanging work sheets or environment becomes humdrum after 180 days. Before the new school year begins, reorganize your classroom, change or put up posters, put fresh flowers in your children's work area. If you are satisfied with your curriculum choice, think about adding supplemental learning material that would benefit certain subject areas and inspire learning. It could make the difference between ending your school year with a bang, and killing it completely.

E = **Earnest.** Being earnest implies caring about the quality of education your child is receiving. "Busyness" before and after school may sometimes find us "schooling for home school's sake" and not paying attention to details. I liked to remind myself that I must be careful to note what is being learned, how learning is taking place, or if any learning is taking place. At day's end, can I conclude that progress has accompanied the time my children and I spent together in class?

Is your "E" for "extracurricular?" Does time away from home appeal to you more than time at home? Do too many outside activities take precedence over your day? However, extracurricular activities help to "round out" our children's time at home. Often, outside activities appeal greatly to both teacher and student. But remember, to have a healthy school, we must balance our outside activities and our home school obligations. Well, that takes care of the word "H - O - M - E." Now what about the "S - C - H - O - O - L?"

S = **Student.** Our students come first, of course! Our students offer us some of the most exciting, challenging and rewarding days we will ever live through. Whatever the ultimate goal for our home school, be it home school through high school years or for just the elementary and middle school years, our students will reap the benefits. If it turns out theirs is a dream to continue the home school tradition with their own families, rest assured that such a decision is often influenced by what we've modeled during the time we taught and trained them.

I occasionally encounter a mom who's had a very difficult or trying year and who would substitute the word **"sorry"** for **"student."** Perhaps you're frustrated or disappointed that your student didn't "soar" academically under your tutelage. I believe one reason home school success stories outweigh stories of home school failure is because many of us who experience failure in certain areas continue on until there is success.

Regret about any poor decisions we've made can only be resolved one of two ways: reverse the decision if possible, or make a conscious effort to make the most of a poor decision by praying for direction out of it.

Whatever the case may be, stick with it until things get better. They surely will.

C = Creative. Keep your classes imaginative and your ideas fresh and resourceful! The Lord has gifted each of us uniquely and abundantly to accomplish great things within our homes, as well as our schools. The privilege of home schooling allows our creative mindset to take flight, be imaginative, and unlimited, as we plan for our school year.

Whatever happens, don't let your **"C" stand for "critical."** We all expect assignments and projects to be done correctly, papers to be neatly written, assignments completed and turned in on time.

However, I know from personal experience, that doesn't always happen. Make your expectations known to your child and encourage him to meet them. Unless you discern a deliberately slothful spirit, sometimes you might have to praise less than perfect work, in order not to be overly critical. Our goal is to be picky teachers, but not pick apart our students.

H = Heart. Is it possible to be with your children day after day unless your heart is in it? Our hearts are entangled in home schooling, not by default but by divine order. It's important that our children realize how deeply we love them and love to teach them—not by giving them a litany of our self sacrifices, but by seeing how much of ourselves, our hearts, we are willing to commit to them.

O = Open. Encourage your children to be open with you. As children grow older, they should be encouraged, even charged with the responsibility through prayer for helping to select their curriculum, academic courses, etc. Knowing how our children feel about a certain curriculum, learning tool, or class schedule will save us time and effort, plus avoid hours, days and weeks of frustration. Frustration is often borne out of a student's lack of freedom to express his ideas and thoughts regarding decisions that directly affect him.

Let's hope your **"O" will never be defined as "obstinate."** Putting off or forgetting to do chores, occasionally forgetting or neglecting assignments, or carelessness when the occasion calls for responsibility is pretty normal behavior for most children, and especially teens. But selfishly demanding privileges, independence or rights, willfully neglecting to give honor to parents, and refusing to submit to parental authority require immediate attention. These are the makings of a rough storm headed toward your home school. Best advice: halt class for the day, or the week, if necessary. Deal with the character issues and obstinate spirit and then continue on prayerfully.

O = Opportunity?" Your home school should be full of wonderful opportunities for education, experience, and exposure for your child. The beauty of home schooling is our ability to enhance our students' learning through a myriad of possibilities.

Keep your child's learning at his own pace, not those of your neighbor's kids, or the children of that most outstanding member of your support group, lest this **"O" for you become "overwhelming!"** Trying to keep up with the astonishing learning abilities of others is not the point of home education.

L = **Listen.** Having our children near us and with us throughout the day is such a privilege. Take time to listen to your children with your ears and your heart. This is one of the most important gifts we can give to them. This "L" should not stand for "lessons." Home school should always be defined as more than lessons.

Learning is important, but worksheets, assignments, and schoolwork are not all there is to school. Field trips, play time, music, read aloud time, special projects and family time should be interspersed throughout your home school days.

There is another "L" word that defines our home school: **love.** Without love, our home and school indeed will become as empty and hollow as *"... a sounding brass and tinkling cymbal." (1 Cor. 13:1b).*

Remember, "Empty" teaching will produce emptiness in spirit.
Teaching from a heart of love will produce a love of learning and help students love school!

Inspiration

Midway through the school year, right after Christmas, and before the groundhog's announcement of spring, home school days seem to drag along. The end of the school year seems unbelievably far away. Oh sure, many of us do have the joy of standardized testing to look forward to...or at least I try to be optimistic and consider it joy. It usually isn't an effective thought; testing in and of itself is enough to make one ponder the virtues of beginning another school day. Even so, once testing has been completed, settling back into the sameness of the class routine is anticlimactic, almost dull, and for some, depressing.

We start off the beginning of the new school year with a bang! Lots of energy! We embrace the excitement for new books to be read and new curricula to be used. Or, if we haven't purchased new books and curriculum, then we certainly have new ideas and approaches for the tried and proven teaching tools we've depended on in the past.

Yet, by January and February, we're retrospective about how school is going: sometimes we're simply dissatisfied with the progress of the school year or our students. You may have a few goals or objectives yet to be implemented, let alone actually achieved. This would be a good time to review them.

Revisiting what you wanted to accomplish at the beginning of the year may serve as inspiration or encouragement now. The fact that we are not quite on target should not serve as condemnation to us or as a flag of failure. Rather, it will help us reevaluate goals and objectives.

Perhaps you're dissatisfied with the materials you've been using or your method of teaching? If you've discovered what you've been using does not fit your teaching style, or your child's learning style, what better time than now to make a change?

So, you may ask, "How do I do it? How will I manage to keep my inspiration long enough to make it to May or June?"

First, I would encourage you to talk with your spouse and share your thoughts or struggles with getting back in the swing of things after the Christmas break and over the dreary winter months. Although your perceptions and viewpoints may differ, a spouse's support for what you are doing and how you are doing it will be invaluable. I assure you that whether or not I've immediately agreed with my husband's assessment of our home school, I have always been grateful to have him offer his support and I realized that his leadership and outlook were an amazing boost for a somewhat withering home school season.

Secondly, sometimes a simple change to our previous school schedule is very helpful. Changing the routine breaks the monotony. We all know there is little or nothing to be inspired about when we're in a monotonous situation. Spring fever does not only affect our children!

Finally, let's always remember to look to the Lord for inspiration. Find your inspiration through prayer and His Word.

Counter the effects of spring fever
by planning special field trips,
family outings or activities
as often as the weather permits
during the long winter months.

Juggle

Defined, juggle means "to handle or deal with usually several things (such as obligations) at one time so as to satisfy often competing requirements." Why does that definition come as no surprise? Further, why does it seem to come easy to moms (or does it?)

Think for just a moment about learning to juggle. How do you start? With just one ball. You throw it up and catch it, throw it up and catch it, until you master catching the ball without looking. For many of us, that would be equivalent to getting married and learning how to be a wife, no matter how much we thought we knew or had been taught.

Then, you add in another ball until you master two. Perhaps this was child number one, hence learning to be a mom. Then slowly you add in another ball, and then another. This stage is where the family is in full operation, so to speak, and you now begin child rearing and start to form traditions and values. As you add a fourth and fifth ball, things start to get complicated and interesting.

When you add home schooling to the cycle of balls, things will spin out of control if you're not careful. It's much the same with teaching our kids. Don't start out your first school year with a too-intense class schedule. Your 1st grade daughter does not need kiddie algebra to make her competitive down the road or to give her an edge.

Start with one skill you are attempting to teach, and when you and your student have mastered that skill, add the next. Give your children the same advantage you had of adding a ball at a time. Home school should not be an overwhelming experience. If you aren't ready to juggle more into your life, chances are, neither are your children.

Here are a few juggling facts:

- If we try to juggle too many things at once, we drop things *(feeling stressed and rushed to complete school or housework or dinner).* We can get careless, our work can get shoddy, and one by one, things can start to fall apart *(no time to check school work or hear confidences moms need to hear).*
- Juggling is an art, plus it looks like a lot of fun. But professional jugglers will assure you that there are many hours of learning just when to add that next ball to the circle.
- When it comes to home education, we as teachers wear many hats, very proudly, I might add, but many hats just the same. The trick, we have often been told, is to keep each of the hats on our heads, no matter what. I think that's a fallacy. It's perfectly all right to remove the "mom" hat at times when you're teaching, just as it is wise to remove the "teacher" hat when your children need you to be mom.

Juggle your schedule, juggle your time, juggle your priorities, but never juggle your students around your pursuits. Give them a sense of feeling special or a priority in your life!

Kids

When it came to writing something for this letter, "K," I had a few ideas, but honestly, they seemed so lame and caused me to try too hard to make the proverbial round peg fit into a square hole. I have a few "experts" (read: home school graduates) currently living with me; one happens to be my daughter. I told her I was stuck on this one letter of the alphabet and needed some help coming up with better words than I had written down. She matter-of-factly said, "kids."

Well, she doesn't know the fear and trepidation I have about using that word, which is why I didn't write it down in the first place. I remember a discussion with a mom years ago, when I casually used the word "kids" referring to either her children or mine. At any rate, she vehemently launched into a protest and was simply aghast that I would "refer to someone's child as a young goat.'"

Whoa, stop the presses! I, of course, had no idea how touchy the subject is for some folks.

Today, however, I'd like to believe that I've matured to the place where I am no longer just referring to someone's "kids," I'm actually writing about them.

Not only did my daughter suggest the word for the letter "K," she also clued me in as to *why* the suggestion. "Mom," she said, "Parents need to let their kids be kids and stop trying to make them be full-time scholars."

Well-stated, I thought, but I was also quick to make sure that's not what she felt her childhood was like—all scholarship and no fun!

We do want our kids to be scholars, but not at the risk of sabotaging their entire childhood. True, we must think about college entrance exams. Or if we plan to stop home school just before high school, we want our student to be ready to enter traditional school at their home schooled level.

Admittedly, there are some parents who are "all work and no play" kind of people. They see no real benefit in allowing kids (their own or anyone else's) time to stop the book learning and the constant competition. I believe, however, if you are doing your due diligence as their teacher, your children will be just fine. Anyway, there are a good number of studies showing that having fun or playing is another way for kids of all ages to learn.

Sometimes, even under the best circumstances and with the best intentions, we unfortunately miss the mark. The point, I believe, is to try your best to be intentional about how hard and how often you press your children to study over play or downtime.

Some days, after a long morning of study, we would take a break and go outside. Weeks after long months of study, I personally would enjoy watching the kids:

Letting off steam:

- Swinging on a tire swing put up by their grandfather (At age 72, I might add) in our front yard
- Climb trees

- Fish in our pond; and attempt to dig their way to China
- Shoot hoops at the basketball goal attached to the garage
- Walk around the block or to the local park for play ground or ball time
- Roller-blading, bike riding; and skateboarding
- Numerous athletic teams: soccer, baseball, basketball, track, football

We also took vacations at the beach and in the mountains.

We won't always understand the antics of our kids. I was pleased and relieved to learn that my friend's children were also guilty of being kids! Sometimes we may actually be at a complete loss to explain what they're saying or doing, or why. It's generally because kids sometimes enjoy:

Wild antics and acting a little weird:

- It's okay if they scream bloodcurdling battle cries or speak in "code" languages that no one but they understand
- Make up jokes or riddles and tell the same one over and over again
- Watch a garden snake chase a mouse, then cheer loudly when the snake wins
- Suck the ketchup straight out of the packet from their favorite fast food restaurant
- Walk around barefoot in the hot sun to see what it was like during the Civil War
- Turn the basement into a "tent city"
- Eat rolled slices of baloney with honey
- Slide down the basement stairs on a snow sled
- Read a college psych book because they're bored

- Stuff their nose with grape flavored floss to block out the smell of a diaper badly in need of changing

As long as they're not doing anything *harmful, illegal or immoral!*

Make your home school and home "the hangout" for fun:

- Have a co-op or enrichment class at your house (if you have the space to accommodate it)
- Roast hot dogs and marshmallows around a backyard fire pit
- Play backyard Flag Football
- Have Movie and Karaoke Nights
- Let them organize Garage Band practices
- Designate Game Nights
- Hang out and do nothing but talk

What did your kids do today that was fun?

Legacy

How will your children remember their home school days? I have learned a handful of things along the way and it's been an exciting and unique (though challenging) journey. It became more adventurous than I ever imagined it would be.

As I moved closer to becoming the mom of home school graduates, I began doing some serious thinking about what I'd done with my own life, and how I impacted my children/students as a mom, teacher, and as a person. My husband and I started out our home school journey with the intention of making each day wonderful (all right, at least good) and meaningful for each of our children.

Every day that we spend as teacher, we are "building our legacy" in either a positive or negative way. You will build a legacy whether you intend to or not. The challenge is always for us to remember this in our daily interactions with our children.

There are a few points I'd like to share to help you nurture and steer your legacy beyond your greatest expectations.

We Tried to Plant Seeds

The seeds of knowledge, empowerment, and overall, the love for learning, were constantly planted and watered with each story read, craft made, class, assignment baseball game, track meet, field trip, spelling bee, board game, support group function, and time spent hanging out with family. Years from now, it will be interesting to see if these are the things that stand out in the children's minds, as they do in mine now. I hope that they will feel that I was willing to teach them whatever they wanted to learn and encouraged them to learn about as many things as they could.

We Tried to Broaden Their Outlook

We were adamant about giving our children large empty boxes, empty paper towel rolls, plastic milk containers, plenty of paint and foil for castle and Viking adventures, balls, ropes, and chalk to help teach them that fun is free and unlimited with the toys of their imagination, and that the imagination is a much better way to spend childhood than watching TV and playing video games night and day.

I want them to remember me with a book in my hand, a book in the car, a book on tape in progress in the car, a book open on the table in the kitchen, a couple of books by the bed, another five books waiting to be read, and twenty books waiting to be returned. At one point, an entire four rows of bookshelf space at our local library was dedicated to the books I placed on hold for my students to read on a weekly basis.

Early on, we determined that we would expose them to other cultures and experiences by traveling as often as we could. We traveled out west while doing a unit study on Transportation and followed the Oregon Trail where pioneer wagons rode, visited the barges in St. Louis and rode an old fashioned luxury steam engine across a mountain gorge. Our students have visited 27 of the 50 states in our country and the District of Columbia. Some of our students have since traveled internationally. All of us have traveled around the world via movies and books. We did this so they could become more understanding global citizens and also recognize where change needs to occur. In the future they may become the change makers.

We Tried to Expand Their Worldview

We felt it was important to teach our students to reach out to others who were disadvantaged or disenfranchised due to their life circumstances. For 60 days we volunteered at a homeless shelter for families, spending Saturday mornings fixing pancakes and sausage for moms, dads and their children. Not trying to be grand and noble, but by learning to reach out compassionately to others, we helped the children understand it could well have been our family in that shelter and that there are people who care. We volunteered with our local food bank, a ministry outreach center, and, of course, in major outreach efforts from our own local church.

We Showed Them Love and Modeled It

My husband and I tried to model love for one another, those within our extended family, church family, and community, by openly expressing it with words, deeds and acts of kindness; and to show our children we really loved them. We loved them enough to set expectations for them, keep consequences, as needed, to give love a balance when disobedience wanted to win out.

These are just a few of the life skills that we trusted would come in handy later when they went their own ways in life.

At the end of the day, my pride in my job and my efforts to improve in it each year are what inspired me to continue home school year after year, especially after the loss of my husband.

Every day that teachers are in the classroom, they are building their legacies. When your students look back as they become the parents of school age children, how will you be remembered?

My prayer for your children, as I've prayed for mine, is that they will take the legacy, which is the baton of your family's life together, and run!

What will your children remember the most about their family journey as they follow you, walk with you, and eventually lead you?

Mastery

Whatever teaching method or approach we use, I feel that it is imperative for us as the teachers to evaluate our children's understanding of the material we've presented during class time. There are many different ways and methods to test your child's mastery of a particular subject, and testing his level of mastery may occur daily, weekly, or monthly. It doesn't really matter; it depends more on the child than anything else. Some children do well with a structured test setting and obviously others don't. The latter may need a less formal approach to finding out what they know or have learned.

For the sake of the reader that is new to home education, I will begin with suggestions which center on the more familiar and simpler testing formats or the types of testing structures needed, if your student was previously in a more traditional setting.

The time-honored written test or exams

These exams may be presented in a number of formats for your child: word definition, matching, comparison, true or false, multiple choice, short answer, or essay questions.

If you are a teacher who prefers to verify your child's mastery by testing, please, please be sure to use some variety in your choices, even if you are using a "canned curriculum" *(purchased curriculum with daily teaching plans and quizzes).* Facing the same type of test all year long would soon be both boring and discouraging. If you devise your own test, try to avoid giving the same type of questions for new subject matter. With preparation and planning, you can structure a simple, yet effective and customized test for your child in a matter of minutes.

Oral

Another method of testing to help us determine our children's mastery or understanding of subject matter is to have them share their knowledge with us in a spoken form. Here's an example from our home school days: during a unit study on "Bridges," our children worked in teams and were given an area of our city to design and construct an imaginary, much needed bridge. Through different phases of the project, each team had to appear before the Mayor and City Council *(my husband and I)* to present its plans for approval. The team leader was responsible for making the presentation, and the team leaders rotated each week. On another occasion, a team of attorneys attempted to plead their cases *(what they'd learned about a particular subject)* before the judge and jury. *(You guessed it - dad and mom again.)*

Another variation on the "oral test" theme is what I used to call our "speed rounds." This entailed each child, when called upon, naming as many facts about an area of study as he could, for example: when we studied about a certain state. Be creative and make it exciting for your students. Utilize a variety of methods over time and identify which one or ones work best for your family.

If your child has problems answering the basic foundational questions for a certain subject, there may be several things going on. First, the material may have been too advanced or difficult for them to process. This may have been presented unclearly in their reading or during class and needs to be covered again. Perhaps the child was not focused or listening. You should also consider the child's learning style versus your teaching style and determine if there are any issues there. The purpose of the testing is to find out how well your child has processed and retained the material you've presented during class, to identify any weak areas, and to analyze the results.

When children feel good about themselves and who they are, it will show in the way they take on, complete, and turn in their assignments. We know when our children have presented their best work to us. We also know when they have been haphazard or careless with the assignments.

Let's face it, many times our children's best efforts may not measure up to our standards, because sometimes our standards are unreachable or unrealistic. We may need to step back from the situation and give ourselves and our children a break, and remind ourselves of the areas of learning our students have mastered.

If you see a pattern of poor work quality, before you criticize their effort or lack of effort, ask yourself the following questions:

- Did I make the assignment and goals for this particular assignment/task clear?
- Does this work reflect the best attempt for my child's level of ability?
- Am I taking the child's failure to have everything right or in order as a personal statement on my ability as his/her teacher?

What a wonderful opportunity to foster a genuine interest and lifetime love of learning in your children!

> Remember, focus on the positive aspects of what your student has mastered and encourage progress, persistence and perseverance. Their pride in their accomplishments will be your sweet reward!

No

My dear friend Dixie used to tell me years ago that she was going to "enroll me in her 'no' class." (It was true; I did not know how to say "no.") It wasn't an actual class of course, but Dixie's wise advice was convicting, convincing and compelling. After stumbling through some remedial learning, I found that saying "no" at the appropriate times was also very freeing.

Getting home

I often found myself wringing my hands about how to complete a task I had signed up for. Whether it was baking cookies at midnight for an activity later on that day, or hastily cutting out material to sew outfits for a performance, it was all just too much. Part of the problem was that I was a habitual procrastinator. Although I still have a tendency to delay, I've learned over the years to become a selective procrastinator. In the early days of my home school, nearly everything from dinner on the table to grading papers was done at the last minute. Might I add here that that practice did nothing to inspire positive family interaction or portray a good example to the children?

I grew up volunteering for a number of service organizations. It was impressed upon me early that volunteering developed character, so I was a scout, a reader at a nursing home, and I helped at our church in many capacities. As a single adult, I volunteered for service organizations, tutored, helped with community gardens, and so on. My husband and I both volunteered our time as a couple to several organizations as well.

As our family began to grow, some of the hours were cut, but not the commitments. I was a volunteer worker for several ministries at our church and was a leader for one or two of them. I served as a helper for all five of our students' classes at least once a month and was also a volunteer teacher for the local Red Cross. Too many irons in the fire began to equal too much time away from the very thing I had prayed to be able to do: spend more time with my family. As we settled into home schooling, I learned that by saying "no" to my individual outside commitments, I was better able to serve my family, and in essence, say "yes" to them.

I've already covered the subject of burnout, but it bears repeating that it's possible to overextend yourself and experience burnout, from doing good things for your community, your church and your home school support group.

This chapter is not intended to discourage you from volunteering. Rather, I hope to offer another perspective on how to say "no" and feel good about saying it; to be positive about exploring those occasions when there exist very good reasons for not offering to volunteer your services or when, at the very least, you need to take a short leave of absence.

Staying there

Volunteering takes time and whether you home school a houseful or an only child, being the teacher is a full time job, not to mention you may be a wife, or care giver for an aging parent, sick child or spouse.

What I learned about being able to live guilt free when I did say "no" is this: there will be stages in your life where you will need to decline any request to volunteer for even the simplest projects. While your children are very young, it's imperative to spend this time nurturing them, sealing the family bond, establishing family traditions, and so on.

I found this to be the case as my husband's health began to decline. I had been in a leadership role for my home school support group for several years, but spending time with him, as well as caring for him, became my top priority.

Remember:

- Recognize when you arc over-committed.
- Don't catch others' enthusiasm and find yourself caught up in their wave to volunteer for something you'll regret later on. We've probably all been in a situation with a friend who says, "I don't think I'd be any good at this by myself, but if you help me...." Love them, offer advice upfront, during their project, or both, but remain firm in your "no."
- Learn to discern the types of projects and activities that you end up feeling "obligated" to participate, lead, or both. If your time does not allow for the project, say so immediately. We've all also been in situations where someone has volunteered to do something and at the last minute had to break their commitment. That throws a monkey wrench in everyone's plans.
- Say no gently but firmly.

One day things became crystal clear as my phone rang very early in the morning. The conversation went something like this: "Good Morning, I wanted to catch you before you started your classes." "Oh, well, you're too late. It's 9 o'clock and we start at 8." "Oh well, do you have 2 minutes?" It went downhill from there as my friend tried to tell me (in her interpretation of what 2 minutes is) about a woman who'd called her because she was stranded, and, you see, she was at work, doing a "real job" (this part wasn't spoken, just implied) and there was no way she'd be able to get away, even for just the 15 minutes she promised me it would take to meet the woman. I felt compelled to help out, because of the compassion I feel for anyone one who is stranded or in any type of traumatic situation. However, I *was* "working at a real job", too! I basically gritted my teeth and said "no."

Remember, you must do what is best for yourself, your family, and your home school. Learning to say no with graciousness and positivity will help take the sting out of declining any offer to volunteer whether as chairperson or as a behind-the-scenes worker. I realized that saying "no" when I needed to did not close all the doors for volunteering during a different season of life. It is your responsibility to protect your time with your family and to make sure that you are available to them when and while they need you the most.

> Let's practice that little word that is often neglected during committee formations, fund raisers, conversations stemming from favor asking, "no, no, no."

ORGANIZED

If you describe yourself, your home and home school as organized, you may skip this chapter. The very fact that I had to write a chapter on organization will give you a clue as to where I fit in this discussion. I considered myself a fairly well organized individual, until I had two children. Then my skills were challenged, to say the least, with cleaning, and trying to stay on top of the laundry.

After we adopted four boys and fostered two girls, we became a family of eight with six children under the age of 9. I switched into what felt like supermom mode with nonstop cooking, cleaning, and mountains of laundry piled in various places around the house, all while working outside the home.

When we decided I should leave the madness of pursuing a career to stay home and home school, I began my book-buying frenzy, coupled with all the necessary school supplies. I felt myself being pushed closer to the edge as we started each day with a scavenger hunt for mates to socks, missing pencils, misplaced notebooks, and so on. The picture perfect home, school, and students was just not panning out quite the way I thought it would. It was time for me to realize that the organization skills I had as a newlywed or the skills we had as a childless couple were never going to work with a large family.

Here are a few lessons I've learned about organization:

- **It takes work.** There is a lot of effort involved with organizing your home just for livability, even more so for setting up a space or room for class. My husband and I quickly abandoned the kitchen table as the central meeting space for classes, and relocated to our family room in the basement. We went to an office supply store and discovered an Executive Computer desk station, essentially a desk with an unusually long L-shaped extension. It was perfect for seating 5 students, and a 6th easily enough when the 6th one grew into it. Now, you may not have a room or extra space to devote entirely as a classroom. In order to avoid the continual classroom spread throughout the entire length and breadth of your house, create a designated storage space for school supplies and work books, etc., so that wherever you hold your classes, the materials are easily retrieved and returned. Doing so will also allow your family to get a break from school and just be just a family again.
- **It takes discipline.** Few are the home school moms who can resist a book sale, or a box marked "Free Curriculum and Resource Materials." We often end up bringing home a few extra books that we've wanted our children to read, and selecting a few pieces out of that curriculum box, not needed now, but perhaps soon. Sometimes the entire box of free curriculum found its way into our van! Unfortunately, while there was usually more than enough room in our van, it was not the case when we brought it into the house. I eventually had to learn to say" no", (and I am still learning.)

- **It takes creativity.** After enough mornings of "he has my pencil" and "those are my notebooks," I decided to assign each child a color-coordinated supply of pencils, notebooks, erasers, and book bag. We pre-purchased their supplies, and on the first day of school, opened up a "school bookstore," allowing the children to do their shopping. For my sanity's sake, I purchased colored hanging folders for my file cabinet to coordinate with each student's selection and, although their color preferences changed from year to year, (most of the time) the folders worked wonderfully well whenever I needed to switch them around. There was ample space beneath each workspace area for them to store the school things, which eliminated the time waster of hunting down their school supplies each day. (It also made the "he's got my pencil" argument go away for good.)
- **It takes time.** Once you have the physical and tangible challenges under control, you'll want to set some priorities and time management guidelines. Busyness is the order of the day, and it seems to be increasingly difficult to commit so many appointments to memory and not to eventually get something mixed up. Someone once shared with me that she'd written down "4 pm" in her day planner with nothing beside it. As the time grew closer to 4 pm, she could not remember the significance of the date or time; she had no clue if she was to be somewhere at 4 pm, or if someone was coming to see her at that time!

  For some families, a central and family calendar works. Class schedules, extracurricular activities, doctor and dental appointments and so on, are placed on it.

  Once you've organized the outside activities and medical appointments, on your calendar, you are ready to begin setting up your class schedule. We often had many of our medical appointments scheduled on the same day. Knowing this in advance helped me to plan lighter classes for those days rather than scheduling biology, for instance, which would need a lab and extra school time.

- **It takes diligence.** I am convinced that nothing will burn you out or discourage you quicker than a backlog of school assignments. Even more, nothing is probably more discouraging to our students than for them to see their school work sitting in a stack of papers day after day. Be diligent about keeping up with assignments.

  Here again, you'll want to set priorities in handling assignments. I quickly learned that trying to teach six separate grade levels all in one day was a fast track to shutting down our home school for good. Somehow, I stumbled across a method of teaching called "unit studies" where all students learn about the same topic. This gave the children things to discuss, which increased their learning outside the classroom, and made it so much easier for me to prepare their lessons. Unit studies were a great help to me.

Organization is key, because even "free spirits" want to find pencils and other supplies without shutting down school for an all out search for missing items.
Organize students, supplies, and school to fit your family's lifestyle and your personality.

Pitfalls

Well, well she exclaimed
Just look at me
My calendar's full
I've no days free
Juggling our classes
I rip and run
I write out long lists
Of plans begun
Most days, school starts late
Or it's not done
I think it's all right
We're having fun!

The home school journey is not without its fair share of pitfalls. Here are a few lessons I've learned along the way from a few pitfalls our school fell into or managed to avoid:

- **My School Versus Your School**

  We are unique as individuals, as families, and as home schools! Even though we are keenly aware of this fact, we still tend to run the comparison tape with other friends who home school, and end up feeling as though we are miserable failures or just don't quite measure up to everyone else.

Whenever we hear or read about yet another home school "student success" story, we often begin to scrutinize the teaching methods of the "successful ones," comparing how much time we put into our school days versus how much they've put into theirs. Then, taking it one step further, we begin to wonder if it's our curriculum that's holding our student back, and, if we switch to what they're using, perhaps we, too, will be able to produce the same successful results. Comparing our accomplishments to other home school families often results in dissatisfaction and discontentment. That will be reflected in our teaching, current curriculum choice, and possibly the direction of our school.

One way to avoid this pitfall is to stay focused on the vision and goals you've hopefully already established for your school. Remember, teaching your children is a wonderful privilege, and your school should reflect the uniqueness of your family's character. We already know—but sometimes forget—that the perfect curriculum, the perfect home school, and the perfect home school student do not exist. So revel in what God has already entrusted in your care; trust Him to help you make the wise choices suitably designed for you and your family.

- **Overcommitment**

  As any good parent would, we strive to ensure our children have every opportunity to become involved in and exposed to extracurricular activities. This seems to be especially true if our children were formerly public or private school students and we are anxious to replace the activities they had before. So why, you may ask, is that a pitfall?

Extracurricular activities in and of themselves are a wonderful way to supplement your student's school experience. The caution is simply to remember to "keep the main thing the main thing."

In other words, determine when and how many extracurricular activities should be added to your student's calendar at the beginning of the year, or perhaps at the start of each semester or school break. It's important to remember that timing is critical. Determining an appropriate time for additional activities will be a good thing for you and your entire family. Let any increase in activity be gradual, rather than leaping into numerous activities all at once. *(See chapter on Random Acts of Teaching.)*

Remember, if you know the direction your home school is headed you will be aware of lurking pitfalls, and learn how to avoid them.

If you don't have any particular direction or destination for your school, the pitfalls will find you.

Quitting

What is this word doing in a book about home school? I imagine some may be shocked, but it happens. I would venture to guess many of us know at least one family that quit home schooling and put the children into a traditional school of some kind, private or public. Now, of course, if someone has already quit home schooling, why would they be reading this book? You're right, they wouldn't. What I want to offer is encouragement and support if quitting is the decision you are in the process of trying to make.

As with anything else, there are as many reasons to quit home schooling your children as there are reasons to start. There seems to be a common mindset that we have to wait for things to get absolutely terrible before we can even consider change. We often read articles that insist it just doesn't make sense to stop home school under any circumstance and that we're to push through. Sometimes pushing through is not an option.

Surely we will all have that experience, where everyone is tired of school, not necessarily "burned out," but losing interest in the home school experience. There are myriad of reasons why your home school journey may be coming to an end.

Of course, if, as you're reading this book, wanting to quit has not yet been your experience, rest assured there may come a day when you will wistfully watch that yellow school bus roll down the street past your house.

In the instance of critical or terminal illness of a child or spouse, the practicality of trying to teach while also being a full time care giver could be overwhelming. I look back on my care giving days when we spent many days doing school in a hospital room while my husband received medical care. Had it not been for good friends who rallied around, offered support, transportation and "on the spot" co-ops, our school would have been shut down.

Sometimes, very unfortunately, there are domestic situations, such as divorce and separation that necessitates home school will no longer be an option, at least temporarily, while families sort things out.

Perhaps your students are becoming curious about what they're missing out on in a public or private school setting, or maybe they are passionate about sports and there is no sports league in your area.

If things are generally going well when suddenly you hit a rough patch, and there seems to be increasing resistance to learning or staying at home; there are other strategies to employ while the "dust is settling," so to speak. Pushing through is not great advice if there are daily battles, and more time is spent arguing, coercing or threatening your unmotivated son or daughter to get on with the business of school.

If everyone is in agreement that the long-term goal for your family is to graduate your student from home school, give everyone a chance to heal from the battle, rather than starting up the war with each new school day. There are times when counseling, whether from your clergy, or other professional counselor is needed. The worst thing we can do is allow our pride to make the decision for us to not find help, either for ourselves, our student or entire family.

Depending on the state requirements and regulations for home educators in your geographic location, put school on hiatus for a couple of weeks to regroup, rethink and refine everything home school.

I feel very blessed in that I've never experienced the constant drama in the classroom that many a mom has contacted me about, on the verge of tears and needing validation to quit. That's not to say we as a family didn't have our fair share of challenges; thankfully, just never to the degree of quitting.

I know the thought of quitting for many is an emotionally charged one. As I look back on the early days of home schooling our brood, I often wonder if perhaps one or two of our children wouldn't have done better returning to traditional school in the later years. I have pondered this as a result of conversations with a few friends and strangers who home schooled their boys. Yet, after much pondering I always come back to the same conclusion; for our family, I believe at the time the right decision was made.

There is a huge difference between quitting and giving up. Giving up may be more of an emotionally based, rash decision. Quitting, I believe, requires more thought. Further, giving up will likely result in never revisiting the option of home school again. Quitting will perhaps leave the possibility of re-opening your school at a future time. There are a number of reasons for quitting or closing your home school. Some are basic and simple (your family initially agreed to stop school after a year); some are much more complicated (personal family issues, e.g., mental health, physical health challenges, behavioral issues, etc.). The decision rests entirely with you and your circumstances.

If you find you need to follow a different plan for your family and your direction has changed, take the Nike motto to heart and "Just Do It."

Random

Oh please let us run
The little boy cried
No give us a rope
To go play outside
But we love to hear
Cheering crowds scream
Clapping and rooting
For us and our team
Games, balls and running
I have no such need
Please, may I go to
The park, sit and read?
Well I have a mitt
I want to play catch
One day I do hope
Our plans will soon match.

Many years ago, when we first began to home school, the "extracurricular" world of home school was almost nonexistent. Activities outside of the home were extremely limited. An art class here, a biology lab there, and a few loosely organized team sports thrown in for good measure seemed to serve the home school community well.

In recent years all of that has changed. Theater groups, organized and competitive sports leagues (not to mention regional and state tournaments for those leagues), co-ops, enrichment classes, debate clubs, chess clubs, bowling leagues, and more are now available to homeschoolers.

It's truly amazing! It's truly exciting! With a simple "point and click," we are able to sign our children up for a myriad of activities and classes outside the home. Yet, I caution you with this sage advice that you "cannot home school in your spare time." No, I was not the wise sage that spoke those riveting words. A dear friend of mine shared what she felt was a very strong impression in her heart from the Lord concerning the number of outside activities she had involved her family in. He wanted her to realize that home schooling in her "spare time" was what she had been doing. Ouch!

So how does one avoid committing random acts of teaching as a result of taking on too many activities outside the home? After all, we do want our scholars to be academically, physically, emotionally, and socially well rounded, don't we? Of course we do, but at what cost? Besides, staying home to teach is part of what gives home education its appeal, don't you think?

The point I hope to make here is that we must weigh each decision for extracurricular activities, lest our desire for giving our children a well-rounded school experience becomes out of balance with the amount of time we're actually supposed to be teaching them.

My own story is somewhat similar. Five boys and one girl makes for a very interesting combination when trying to decide which outside activities to pursue. Football, basketball, softball and other organized sports leagues for home school students were still non-existent when our children were younger, and in our state, the option of home school students playing sports with the local public school teams was, and still, remains unavailable.

So we opted to enroll three of our boys on the city's basketball league: big mistake! Rather than put at least 2 of our boys on one team since their birth dates were within a year or two of one another, they each ended up on three separate teams, which means three separate practice and game schedules, and sometimes even different locations! It makes my head spin just to remember the dizzying schedule we kept up for four months trying to make practices and games.

During that time, my husband and I sometimes drove past one another on the road, on our way to games at opposite sides of the city, he with three children and I with the other three. Our school time suffered and was often abbreviated on days these practices and games took place because of the travel time involved.

Following that experience, I entered a phase of letting one child pick a sport, or interest, and pursue it while the rest of the family waited for them to finish the season. Please read that sentence very carefully; I did not write "waited patiently." School and classes thrived, but character traits became unpleasant. After one season, there was such a hue and cry of "I'm bored," "when's it going to be my turn," "I'm tired of watching," etc., etc. So we worked on developing character and moved on to my next big idea.

I began to look for activities that the entire family could become involved in and enjoy. I found a swim instructor who was willing to teach six students plus mom in private swimming lessons. That was a wonderful experience, but it was an outdoor pool, and needless to say the lessons terminated when the season changed.

One of my sons expressed interest in running, so I contacted a local track and field club and enrolled all six children.

There were plenty of activities for each them to choose from; relay races, long distance running or short distance sprinting; high jump or long jump; discus or shot put throwing, etc. That idea lasted for about a year, and it was great; everyone left the house together and came home together. The only problem was that everyone did not like track and field activities.

Happily around this time, the concept of forming sports leagues for home school students began to evolve. There was a soccer team forming for the elementary and middle school grades, which perfectly fit. We tried soccer; it was a lot of fun and everyone enjoyed it. The children became fast friends with other home school students, and some they are still in contact with to this day.

As the children grew older, some became more specialized in the sports they truly enjoyed, and the others decided they were not interested in sports, but a chess or debate league, etc. Then we were back at square one, trying to fit everyone's interests into our school schedule. One day it dawned on me; I was taking the wrong approach to the whole extracurricular issue. The point was not to decide *how* to fit something into our schedule, but to determine *if* anything else needed to be fit into our schedule.

I learned that simply because an activity is offered does not mean we have to jump on the bandwagon and be a part of it. Praying for discernment as to which activities we needed to participate in became and remains a priority for me. Like my friend, I understood the danger of over commitment, I recognized the difficulty of running to this activity and to that place, and the frustration of being too tired to teach, or the children being too tired to listen, or learn. I continued to back away from outside activities that do not answer at least three questions in my mind:

- Does he or she possess a passionate interest or just a passing interest?

- Does he or she have a realistic potential to excel if they pursue it?
- Will adding this activity overload my child's emotional or physical endurance?

Remembering that God has entrusted us with the vision and balance for our family and school, as parents, we must be very selective with our choices and loyal to our calling to disciple, train and educate our children.

I have identified three key areas that have helped me to stay on track as I consider outside activities for my students during the school year.

Commitment

We should have a commitment to assume the responsibility for our school and scholars, to help each family member from being overwhelmed or burned out because of too much shuttling from one activity to another. We must have a greater commitment to supplement or enhance their learning experience with outside resources only when necessary, not simply because they are offered or affordable. Becoming overly involved can become a pitfall, especially to those new to home schooling. I was certainly not against giving my children the broader experience of adding into our schedule classes and activities that provided opportunities to interact or compete with other homeschooled students. I was committed, however, to enjoying this gift of teaching them at home.

Consistency

The word "random" means haphazard, or without direction. That being the case, then surely one of the opposites of that would be the "consistent," meaning fixed, firm, or solid. Our teaching, our classes, and our schedules should follow some logical sequence or daily order, even if known only to our family. Once we have established a regular course of procedure for our school, it is often better to stick with it—at least the first couple of months or a semester—rather than continuing to add to our schedule as new offerings come to the fore.

Our families are likely to suffer, with extreme results, during the school year if we continue to seek outside activities to add to an already full plate. It is one thing to find at the end of the school year that the textbook had not been completed. It is quite another to find mid-year that the workbook had not yet been *opened*.

Control

Many of us determine before our school year begins or our school day starts, exactly what we will teach. Our pre-planning during the summer helps us to decide what to teach and our curriculum greatly dictates it daily or weekly. Before you actually begin your school year, take the time to prayerfully consider, as a family, how much time you want to spend together as a family, and how much time you are willing to share with others.

I'll admit that, in the fall, when all of the home school e-loops are buzzing with announcements for upcoming activities and classes, I wanted to sign up for nearly every one that is listed! I wanted to ensure that my students didn't miss out on lifetime opportunities or experiences.

However, I was committed to being consistent in the teaching and order of my school day. Therefore, I had to strive to exercise control over the tendency to overbook my family and our school time.

Remember, efficient and economic use of your time is important, and so is being able to determine whether or not it is the right time to broaden your child's schedule to include more extracurricular activities. Are they substantiated in light of your philosophy of education? Are the extra activities necessary and desirable for the child's academic growth? Or are we simply going through the motions because others around us are involved in something?

> Remember, having our children at home with us is a fleeting gift.

SUPPORT GROUPS

You must join our group
She implored

You'll not believe all
That's in store

Moms and their families,
There's food galore

Field trips, and play dates
And so much more

Support group, my friend?
"Oh, dear," said I

You want me to join?
And to comply?

Make a commitment?
No, no, not I

We're doing just fine
Was my reply

Please give it more thought
Is what she said

No quick decisions
Think first instead

Planning alone
Is what you do dread
Why not let others
Help you instead?

Once upon a time, I felt that we would be the exception to the rule when it came to joining support groups. After all, our six children were never really without at least a couple of playmates among themselves. I planned each of our many field trips to coordinate beautifully with the beginning or completion of a unit of study. Support groups were for the unimaginative and dependent. I was invited time and again to attend several local support group meetings, all of which I naively declined. We were doing just fine.

Then one day, after many months spent in our classroom and very little interaction with anyone who was actually home schooling, I began to feel very isolated and overwhelmed. I had hit a bump in my perfect road and found I had no one to whom I could go and ask what I felt were pressing questions about something I wanted to teach. I needed advice. We were novices and had not surrounded ourselves with experienced home school families to help us navigate the tide of uncertainties that accompany home education. Although my husband was a pastor at a church just one city over, and we were obviously involved in ministry, at that time there were no other families within our congregation that taught their children at home. The few home school families we did know were mere acquaintances. My closest relationship with any home school family was through a book written by a well known home educator, someone I had never met.

Enter home school reality: I realized that we needed to extend our circle of friends, so we began researching home school support groups in our area. We sifted through the support group listings and their descriptions and made a few calls. Applications, membership requirements, group composition, and demographics were our criteria for choosing which groups to visit. When we finally made the decision to join one group after attending several meetings, we remained in the group for over nine years; I was in a leadership capacity for eight of the nine. It goes without saying that it was a great God-led decision, and not only did we have field trips and activities galore, several lifelong friendships were forged.

Home school support groups provide encouragement and guidance for many home school families. The opportunities to receive advice, tips and wisdom from folks that have had similar experiences are innumerable and invaluable. Lasting friendships often develop between members of home school support groups.

Families that have home schooled for several years are considered veterans and often provide the support and backbone for a group. However, it is not unusual to find groups that have been formed by families new to home schooling. The reasons we join, leave a current group, or start a new support group are as varied as the reasons we choose to home educate our children.

There are groups that support a myriad of home education ideologies and philosophies, religious preferences, ethnicity, gender, age, geographic location, special interests, special needs and/or even hobbies. Bear in mind, the list is nearly endless and this represents an abbreviated overview of the many types of groups that exist.

What does your family need? When surveying your family's needs, ask yourself, "What are my priorities or criteria for joining a particular group?" Is interaction with other moms at the top of your list? Is the issue of socialization a great concern? What about the need for regularly scheduled events? Would you like for your children to participate in scholastic competitions as part of a group? What is the level of commitment required by your family to participate with the support group's activities? For many support groups, attendance at a percentage of activities is required. These are just a few of the questions that will help you avoid becoming overwhelmed and over-committed.

Some support groups exist solely to cater to the needs of the child and are often very activity-driven. There are numerous opportunities to meet playmates, take field trips, etc. This type of support group tends to have larger numbers of pre-school and elementary school age children in it. The group is likely to meet often, since the emphasis is not as heavily on academics and long hours of study (which occurs as the students enters the high school years).

Other support groups focus on the benefit to the parent-teacher. This type of group sponsors activities such as workshops, monthly teacher meetings which focus on skills, confidence building, fellowship and curriculum exchanges, to name a few. It operates more as a ministry of encouragement to moms.

Another example is a support group that is completely family oriented, with activities planned and scheduled to include the entire family. Meetings are held less frequently, usually during the evening hours or on weekends, in an effort to accommodate the work schedules of the dads.

Though not an exhaustive list, here are a few significant points to ponder as you consider which home school support group to join:

Differences between support group offerings:

- Some groups operate as a ministry or under the umbrella of a local church
- Some groups collect dues for membership. Others may require a yearly application fee
- Some groups offer lending libraries or other resource programs
- Some groups publish a newsletter, e-zine, or a yearbook

- Some groups offer co-op or enrichment programs
- Some groups offer athletic leagues, bands, and choirs

Differences in support group administration:

- Some groups have annual rotating leadership, or limit the office of President to a defined term
- Some groups operate as small corporations, with a board of directors, holding annual elections for officers
- Some groups are very laid back, and meet only on an as needed basis
- Some groups are limited to 10 or fewer families in order to maintain intimacy, while others have as many as 300 families in membership
- Some groups maintain a waiting list and continue to accept applications throughout the year, while others will not accept any applications once their quota is filled

The key to finding the right support group is discovering what they do exceptionally well and matching it to your expectation. In this way, it will have significant and continued positive results on your family. So take your time. Visit several groups. Talk with leadership and members before making a choice. Prayerfully consider what type of group your family needs before you make a commitment to join.

Remember, your family does not have to "go it alone." If you don't find the type of support group to fit the needs, characteristic and personality of your home school, consider starting a group!

TESTING

The beginning of spring signals standardized testing for many home school students. I'd like to offer the following pointers:

"Be prepared!"

I remember that saying as the Boy Scout motto, from my older brother's scout days. The point of that message rings just as true today as it did back then. In order for our children to have the best opportunity to do well, we must help them to prepare. Make certain that your children have plenty of rest the day before the actual testing begins. As a rule, children should certainly go to bed on time, and during testing if possible, just a little earlier than usual. Curtailing a few extra activities a couple of days prior to testing is also not a bad idea.

If your child is part of a group and must travel to a testing site, give everyone plenty of time to get started in the morning. Have everything packed into a book bag or in one place. This will help you avoid looking all over the house for missing items, and will help you and your child avert stress. Try to arrive a little early to allow the child a few minutes to settle in or wind down *(but not too early, because the wait may tire the child).* Nourishment is also very important. Don't allow your children to take their tests on an empty stomach.

Help your child to relax.

I think we would all agree that attitude plays a major role in test taking. Remember, your child's attitude will greatly affect how he performs on the test. Your child may want to discuss the purpose or need for taking a standardized test. By all means, talk with them about it, particularly if you notice that the child seems overly concerned with his/her ability to do well on the test.

Help your child approach the test with confidence. Try not to make testing the center of family discussion prior to the event.

Focusing primarily on test results might possibly build undue stress in your child, especially if he senses nervous tension or anxiety in us. As children's teachers, we must be confident of the job we have done as teachers and of what our children have learned. We have already evaluated their skills by various methods throughout the year. We know the areas in which they have strengths and weaknesses.

The testing environment is as important in preparation as any other. Take control of your testing environment. Minimize all obvious and controllable distractions. Help your child or children find a quiet place. If your child is easily distracted, sitting him by a window where he can see all the activities in the neighborhood is not a good idea.

If you have younger children, restrict their play area and playthings to a certain room or part of the house during the test time.

If you test your children at home, make sure that your children understand what time you expect to get started with the tests, remembering again that rushing through the house looking for misplaced items will cause stress. Place everything that your student will need in one central location the night before. Pencils, erasers, and scratch paper should be readily accessible to your student. If you use a computer for the testing, be sure all of the CDs are in one place and ready for use. Small breaks should be given at appropriate times during the test. This is also a great way to limit stress and anxiety. During breaks, provide your child with a light snack. Let them get up, walk around, and stretch. Encourage your child to do their best and not to worry about the end results of the test.

Alert family and friends that you will be testing on certain days and times, and ask that they not call during those hours unless absolutely necessary. Let your voicemail take the message.

The children are prepared! We must help them approach their test with confidence. Although standardized testing is required in many states, I do not believe we should allow it to become the sole method by which we evaluate our child's knowledge or performance on any subject matter.

Again, there are many reasons why some children excel at test taking, and some do poorly; even when we've taken the care to prepare them emotionally, be mindful of their environment, prepare them educationally.

Remember, give your child the greatest advantage and benefit before testing:
much preparation,
little pressure!

Unit Studies

Long before I became a seasoned and much wiser home educator, I attempted what no home mother should ever attempt to do; develop and prepare lesson plans in order to teach multiple grades to multiple children during the course of one day.

Looking back over those early days, I have but one question, "What was I thinking?" Our school day started at 7:45 am and ended somewhere around 9:00 pm. My life did not feel nor did it reflect, one of those picture-perfect home school families plastered on the cover of the home school magazine, which only months earlier had provided me with such joy and inspiration.

What exactly was wrong with this picture?

Those "teachable moments" were becoming quite elusive while, as a matter of fact, so were my children. I'd teach, then we'd pause for lunch, then I'd teach some more, and we'd pause for dinner. The problem actually started somewhere between after dinner and the call back to start school. The main part of our house is circular in nature, so if I called a certain child, we could spend the better part of a minute walking in circles looking for one another. And that's the way my home school was starting to feel. Once the walking stopped, there was that look in our eyes of wanting to bolt. It said, "Please, no more school." Did I mention both teacher and student bore that expression?

About the 5th week into our school year, I stumbled upon some information about the ease with which one mom was teaching all of her eight children the same subjects during the same time.

Enter: unit studies.

To be able to teach all of my six children at one time on the same one topic, such as a period in history, a specific event, or study of fictional or historical characters, was a tremendous blessing to me. My students seemed to be more interested in this type of learning togetherness than with all individual lessons. For some of my students, being able to learn math or science in the context of a study on Egypt made all the difference in the world in terms of holding their interest and learning.

Initially, I learned about unit studies from someone who designed her own, and I thought I'd join that merry band. It did not take me long to realize that, although it was a lot of fun, it was also a lot of work. The amount of time it took for me to research and then write out each grade level's lesson plan began to eat into my day. After my first design of my own unit study, I was through.

Say what you may, but there's a huge advantage to using preplanned curricula when you don't have the luxury of time on your hands, so we decided to purchase a unit study curriculum.

At any rate, the other primary benefit I realized is that having a single source for several topics made lesson planning and teaching easier and simpler, especially in the format developed by the curriculum, because there were fewer resources to deal with. Also, I discovered the unit studies' approach gave my children both in depth and broad understandings of subjects revolving around an entire theme. Again, this really held the interests of the children, especially when we studied the Civil War. So great were their interests that the study went on for two years, as we expanded on a theme far beyond what the unit study, or even I, could have imagined, when visiting numerous Civil War reenactments in several states. We even traveled to Illinois to visit Abraham Lincoln's birthplace. I was not sad when the study ended.

But I digress. If you have multiple ages in your family, and they are as close together in ages as mine were, consider giving unit studies a try. There are a variety of packages available, and don't forget there is the option of designing your own. I must add that, while I initially shied away from designing a study after that first disastrous attempt, I did eventually begin to add to the curriculum. Several times during the course of our home school years, I managed to design a unit study on a few themes the children wanted to learn.

Here are a few of the favorable reasons the unit studies worked for us:

- Our children of different ages and different levels were able to learn together.
- The curriculum came as a K-6 and 7-12 package, so it was relatively low in cost, especially considering the cost of multiple curricula for multiple grades
- I believe our students moved from each study with an in-depth understanding of each topic. Unit studies are designed to be learner-generated
- This particular curriculum allowed each student to work at his own pace, without holding any of the other students back. This helped them to develop mastery of a subject before moving ahead

- Since there are no time restraints, the child is given ample time to think, experiment and discover each topic through his own natural way of learning
- I noticed by their strong finish on quizzes and exams that some of my students, who were special learners, were now better able to understand and retain what they had learned

If the thought of blended learning and learning one theme at a time appeals to you, I encourage you to research and even experiment with a unit study or two before you decide.

If you are interested in learning more about unit studies, your local library and certainly the internet will have a plethora of information available to you.

> Don't be afraid or concerned about experimenting with a variety of curricula. Finding the "right" fit for your students is one of the most important decisions you will make for your school.

Volunteer

When I mentioned cutting down on outside activities and learning the art of saying "no", I also learned that I did not have to give up volunteering altogether; that there existed as many, if not more, opportunities, activities, and projects for us to volunteer for together. That excited me.

I will say that the atmosphere in our home seemed to calm down almost immediately; after we stopped running around and, over time, the new normal for us was making plans for volunteer activities rather than hearing about something and trying to make an on-the-spot decision.

We volunteered several times a year for various projects; the children amassed numerous community service hours, all within the confines of a fairly smoothly running school.

Let me spend a little time here discussing another aspect of volunteering as a family or helping your children with community service hours. Colleges and universities are not solely interested in a student's GPA (Grade Point Average) anymore; they want to ascertain from the transcript how well rounded a student is, and what he or she brings as assets, apart from what they've learned academically. Community service hours listed on the college application provide a quick picture of the type of involvement the student had during the high school years. What's more, they give a window into the personality and interests of the applicant. Over all, the admissions officer hopes to determine a little about how the prospective student will contribute to campus life.

Your student's outside activities with sports teams and other clubs are equally as important, but not to be confused with the weight given to community service hours. If your student has been involved in numerous outside activities, the admissions officer is primarily interested only if the student played a very substantive leadership role and if there was a pattern of longterm involvement in just a few activities. Community service does not necessarily give an edge to any student's application; it is just one of the components that will make it stand out. However, it hurts a student to have no community involvement, since he/she will pale in comparison to other applicants.

In short, most colleges like to see how prospective students view social responsibility to their community and the world. Quality community service projects are just one of the gauges by which it's measured. Side note: don't forget to keep track of all your student contributions.

Here are a few suggestions for helping your family or your student say "yes" to volunteering for something that will help build character, open opportunities, and go on their resume, all in one fell swoop:

Presidential Service Awards

Community service medals recognize volunteers' efforts with bronze, silver and gold. My students especially liked receiving the signed certificate and having a couple signed by various U.S. Presidents. Specifics and details for the program can be found on the website: *www.presidentialserviceawards.gov.*

For many years, our family participated in this program. It is open to families and individuals, which means your student could participate solo. The hours for volunteer service are accrued over a 12 month period.

There are too many places to list where we volunteered over the years, but these were among our favorites, and so, we said "yes" more frequently: thrift stores, local food banks, homeless shelters, nursing homes, libraries, missions, hospitals, ringing the bell for the Salvation Army at Christmas, collecting donations for the Foster Care Angel Tree in an area mall, delivering turkeys to needy families in our church community, etc. We served as a family in some, and others worked out better for our individual students.

Opportunities for your student's and families' growth and development abound with volunteer and community service projects!

Wonder

"O Lord my God, when I in awesome wonder, consider all the worlds thy hands have made!" Those words, from one of my favorite hymns, helped me to understand how and why questions are formed in my children's minds, because we, as adults, do not always clearly understand so many of the complexities around us.

I believe that it must please the Father very much when we are awestruck with wonder at His creation: the moon, the stars, the Earth we live on, and the amazing things He has placed here for us to enjoy.

Furthermore, I am certain He is pleased when we are able to nurture this same type of curious nature in our children. Knowing how to stimulate wonder about our Creator and the things He has created in the world around us for our children to see, feel, smell, enjoy and discover is one of the greatest joys and challenges of teaching our own.

So how do we encourage the natural curiosity of our children? The old adage "curiosity killed the cat," is just that— a bit antiquated. Yet there were some days this teacher was more than challenged to address six times too many questions of "why?", "how?" or, "what if?"

Here are three major points to help you make it through the days when there seem to be more questions than hours for school:

- **Encourage your child to ask questions**

  "Why" is the most familiar word in the vocabulary of a child who is naturally curious. "Why" is a one-size-fits-all kind of question. Our children of all ages just want to know about everything. One question beginning with the word "why," more often than not, leads to another "why," and another, and another.

  With small children, this type of leading question helps them to formulate their ideas and opinions, as well as develop logical thinking patterns.

  Granted, there are some questions we don't always judge as equally valuable strictly in the light of their learning. I will be the first to admit there were some days when 10 "hows," or "whys," multiplied times six children, would seem to push me over the edge. There will be those days when we will all become question weary. With prayer and much patience, however, we will actually be able to encourage them to ask questions about anything and everything.

  A child who feels comfortable consulting his parents about a bug that crawls and doesn't hop, or one that flies instead of rolls, will hopefully become a young adult who, with confidence built on positive past experience, seeks his parent's advice on academics, as well as the weightier matters of life, i.e. social, cultural and spiritual. In other words, he remembers receiving a kind or helpful answer to his questions.

  Based on a solid relationship with the Father, we can show our children how our life's questions and curiosities are answered in His Word, helping them to become rooted and grounded in their own faith. Then, by developing that type of independent dependence, if you will, they will also know to go to His Word as the final authority for their own answers.

Isn't that a major part of our goal, to direct the spiritual search for all of their thoughts, questions, and curiosities towards the Bible, and godly resources?

- **Empower your child**

  Charlotte Mason (1842-1923) was a strong proponent of home education at the turn of the 20th century. She was sure of the necessity of awakening a responsive stir to the divinely implanted principle of curiosity in the young soul. Mason used to say, "The child wants to know." In other words, learn how to allow the child's natural curiosity and their instinctive love of "why" to become a springboard for learning.

  One does not have to spend hundreds of dollars to provide a school full of learning resources. One of the greatest resources available to us, and absolutely free, is our own backyard. Backyard or no, we all certainly have access to a local park.

  Providing an atmosphere in our home that empowers our child to ask questions and make discoveries is crucial, and it is also very easy to do! We can accomplish this by structuring an environment for learning in our home with books and reference resources from internet websites to purchased CDs. Don't forget that old adage: "one man's junk is another man's treasure." Yard sale and thrift stores often prove to be a treasure trove to the curious mind of a child.

- **Reward your child**

  Reward your child's questioning curiosity with a sincere and truthful response. On the days that are long, and patience short, try to avoid a sarcastic remark or indifferent answer that might discourage or wound the one that asks. If the teacher doesn't always know the answer, it's all right; just admit it! We have assumed the responsibility for teaching our children at home because we love them, not because we know everything. I have learned that the question I could not answer has often opened the door to a quick unit or mini study or special project.

Reward your child by showing that you are interested in what they want to know. Above all else, assure your child that no question is too unimportant to warrant your time. Lastly, never stop learning as teacher. I don't know about you, but I was always curious to find out new ways to make learning a great adventure for my children.

> Encourage, motivate, and stimulate your child's natural curiosity by allowing him to ask questions, whether the questions are related to his current topic of study or not.

X

There are few words that begin with "x" that have a practical application to home school. One definition for "x" is "an unknown variable." There are many unknowns when it comes to home schooling, e.g., "How will my children, family, neighbors and friends react when they learn of our decision to home school?" Here is a word beginning with "x" to consider:

Xerophilous - If we apply the first few words of the definition of this word that describes a plant, we would read "thriving or adapted."

What a wonderful goal and complement it is to our home education efforts to observe how well our children thrive and adapt in the home school environment we create for them.

What causes them to thrive? I believe plenty of hands on, supplemental learning activities, field trips and trips to the library will hopefully whet their appetite for more of the same.

Students who have been exposed to public or private school are well able to adapt to their new school if we, through wisdom, create a home school environment conducive to adaptation and growth, not by bringing school home, but by developing a school unlike any other, just like our own home.

The unknown variable is left to God, He is already familiar with the paths that will be taken and the decision made. Your student's path may be a rocky climb for a few years, or a smooth, sure one. Either way, we continue to water and encourage steady growth, leaving every result up to God.

Remember, our children will choose their paths; we will give them every opportunity to thrive!

Yes

This is the second one word class I learned I needed to take almost simultaneously with the "no" class. The difference being this was a self-instructed class. I'm a quick learner.

Remember earlier in the book I stated that by saying "no" to numerous opportunities that would take me away from home, I was in essence saying "yes" to my family? It indeed worked out to be true.

We now had time to relax more on weekends and had some much needed downtime, rather than looking for space on our calendar to do the things we wanted to do. I recognized the power that came with being selective about how I spent my time as a volunteer and that, while helping others was important, spending time with family was more important. Being available to help, love and enjoy them were blessings. This is a message I continue to share with others.

I also learned about how good you feel when you say "no" to the things that were out of time for your season of life or your family's, and how wonderful it felt to say "yes" to the right things, people and projects. What I'm talking about here is:

- To make a conscious decision to pay more attention to my family

- To have the time to shape and develop my children's core values toward family, community, nation, and God
- To be excited to have more energy
- To be more than just physically present during home school hours *(when you're tired the emotions seem to drain first)*
- To be happy to be the influence in my children's lives rather than a sitter
- To be grateful for the time to provide what they needed, when they needed it *(I was also much more inclined to say "yes" to my children's requests for more of my time)*

Family time gave more opportunities for us: to talk after school or late at night; to help with extra projects or problem subjects; to join in baking cookies, or, to take reading together, extra field trips, and to just hang out or play.

I cannot begin to tell you all the benefits and what I have learned from saying "yes" to family time. The bottom line is, our children will grow up and move away. Whether that move is clear around the globe or just down the street, one day they will be gone.

When your children launch into their own life journey, it will leave you with plenty of time to pursue personal interests of all types. So, for now, please consider the consequences and invest your "yes" into your family. Enjoy your time with them now!

Zowie

The word "zowie" is "used to express astonishment or admiration especially in response to something sudden or speedy." This is the exact word I would use to describe our home school journey. In retrospect, the time has literally sped by, and I've cherished the journey.

There were very few "firsts" I actually had to miss out on in the brief time our children were enrolled in school outside the home. Generally speaking, an eighteen-year journey does not happen so quickly that one would ask where the time went. If it did, it would leave most people emotionally, physically and spiritually drained. I am not. The experience has left me satisfied; content and more convinced than ever that home education was the right option for our family.

Are you considering home school and not certain of how things will turn out? To you I say, "go for it" and trust the journey and outcome to the Father. He's the only One who really knows the end results. Have you already started your home school journey and wonder if you'll make it to the end, whatever that looks like for you?

I say, "Reach for it, take heart," and enjoy your journey. Home school is a privilege, responsibility and opportunity. We as parents lay a foundation for our children, upon which they are able to build for the rest of their lives. We are blessed to prepare them to become good, productive citizens in their communities and the Kingdom. Home school is not a guarantee that, as our children move into adulthood, all of them will make good decisions and do well. Sadly, they may not take the path we desire for them or the one they know is best for them.

On the other hand, one day in the future, you may have the pleasure of your adult children working with you in a business venture, serving with you in ministry, or just doing life with you.

That's joy!

Conclusion

Writing about the blessings of home school today, and remembering a season of extremely difficult circumstances, reminds me of how it presented a major challenge to my faith, in God, educational choices, and expected future results. Struggling (wrestling) to teach during that long ago season has caused me to wonder if this is how Jacob, in the Bible story, must have felt during his wrestle with the angel. Although I'm no longer in the throes of it, I have certainly been able to relate to that wrestling match. It all happened during a time school was not finished, but certainly came to a grinding halt. I have learned, and am convinced that, if I maintained my focus and managed by the grace of God, not to walk away, I could expect the same result as Jacob. There is a blessing to be conferred upon me as well.

On a day, a few years ago, when I did not feel blessed or notice any particular benefit being derived for either teacher or student, this thought suddenly occurred to me: celebrate what has already been produced and accomplished with your students. Keep your expectations (read: *faith*) high for that which has already been sown. After all, the results are God's responsibility, not mine. In keeping with this line of reasoning, I have learned over the years to align my thoughts along these three principles:

Reasons

Why in the world am I home schooling?

Were I to poll at least half of the families I know that home school and ask each of them to name just one reason for their decision to home school, I am guaranteed none of them would share the same reason. We may share many similar experiences that helped to influence and shape our decision to home educate our children. However, the reason that ultimately led to our final decision will be unique to us. I am certain this same thought, to an extent, rings true for my friends that have placed their children in public and private schools.

As home educators, apart from the obvious educational preference, the bottom line is we want to plant into the hearts of our children/students morals, values, family culture and a worldview consistent with what we as parents believe represents God's plan for our lives. Over the past 18 years, quite a few of our original reasons for home schooling morphed into lifestyle and family culture rather than single definitive reasons to home teach.

Reflecting and rejoicing over the reasons we home school strengthens our resolve to stick with it. Remember, Jacob in his struggle was victorious after all. We are still sowing diligently during these times of struggle

Reaping

During the autumn we witness bountiful harvest across the land. There are field trips to farms, pumpkin patches and farmers' markets, as well as, outings to local, county and state fairs. This is a time for gathering a tangible reward for those who have invested time and labor in order to produce a crop. **It is a wonderful time of celebration** for the one that labored to observe the fruit of his efforts. It allows the farmer a chance to bask in the joy that comes from a bountiful crop that will provide food for his family and many others over the coming months. And so it is with those of us who teach at home.

Talk about labor intensive! From what little I know about planting crops and farming, it involves **early rising,** lots of soil **cultivation,** the **planting** of the crop, the **continuous care** of the crop in its varying stages, and finally the **harvesting** of the crop. The analogy here is very clear.

Reward

The greatest and most coveted prize at any county or state fair is receiving the blue ribbon!

Let's think back to the many months prior to receiving this prize. To begin with, let's say a farmer has planted wheat for many years. With the planting of each new crop, the farmer has a vision of how the crop is going to grow and mature. The hope and principle is that if he consistently follows sound practices for sowing and caring for his crop as he has in the past, the activity that brought him success in the past will bring a successful crop once again. There are no guarantees though. He may face a year that brings flood or drought. There may be an unprecedented attack of aphids or armyworms. Each of these occurrences has the potential to destroy **everything** the farmer has worked so hard to produce. Furthermore, the farmer cannot, try as he might, control any of these natural disasters.

I use this analogy as a point of encouragement. The blessings and benefits of being the sower/teacher of our children allow us to work towards a God-directed vision and clearly stated goals. We attempt to sow academic, social, cultural, and spiritual seeds into their lives. If we have home schooled more than one child, we rely on successful past experiences to help guide the process. If we have only one child, or are new to home schooling, we tend to look around at what others are doing and mimic what they are doing (so to speak).

The challenge of being the sower/teacher for our children is that 1st grade or 5th grade or 11th grade may be the year of drought or flood or unprecedented attacks for your school or family. Circumstances beyond your control may seemingly completely ruin your "crop." Rare is the farmer who'll say "that's it for me" after losing an entire crop. Rather, he will wait until the difficulty is abated, and in the appropriate season, begin to plant again. Much like the farmer, we continue to plant, water, and care for our crops despite the difficult, discouraging school days.

Whether you see it or not, believe there is a wonderful harvest ahead!

Questions

Question: *Let's just say it's not been a great year—certainly not what my expectations were. I feel like I have failed in some areas and floundering like a fish out of water. I'm dealing with a child who cheats on her quizzes/tests. What can I do?*

Answer: I would suggest spending time with your child and on your knees. Stop classes for the next few days. Speak to your student and address the cheating. This is a character and heart issue, and it's impossible to teach class if you haven't reached your child's heart. Do some fun family projects and help the child open up to you so you can discover (with prayer) the root cause of her cheating.

Question: *I am considering home schooling again—now more than ever—because I have had it with my children's school. It is very difficult for me because my husband is totally against it. I do not want to start something like this and not stick with it.*

Answer: Home school totally engulfs a family to the point that it no longer is merely an educational choice, it becomes a lifestyle. It would be difficult if not nearly impossible to home school without the consent and support of your spouse, from both a biblical and pragmatic standpoint.

I would suggest you not move ahead with your plans until you both agree it is the right decision for your family.

Question: *My husband and I have decided to go through with home schooling, but we need our hands held a bit to build the confidence necessary to do it the right way without a lot of mistakes (why reinvent the wheel or miss the mark?)*

Answer: Congratulations! Read as many books on home education as are available to you through your library, on-line, or perhaps borrowed from friends. If you currently have friends who home school that is a great advantage. If you do not, find a listing for your state home school organization and ask for a listing of local support groups. Attend several meetings and hopefully, in the process, you will meet someone you'd like to have as a mentor. By the way, you will not home school without a few mistakes, same as parenting.

Question: *Oh no Lord, please, really I should have thought more about what we were getting into, maybe I was not ready—ever! Is this really how my life is going to be for the next 18 years? My normal life seems over!*

Answer: Your question made me smile. I know life during this season seems a bit overwhelming, and sometimes it is. Let me assure you, as time goes by, and you become settled into the home school lifestyle you will be surprised at how easy it becomes. Ask the Lord for daily direction and, if you are not part of a home school group or know other home school moms to compare notes with, contact your state home school organization. Realizing what your expectations are for home school will help you envision what your family would like your home school journey to look like over the next few years. Also, take time to write out your educational goals and a mission statement for your home school.

Question: *All of my friends seem to be traveling and free, while I'm confined to my house with children, performing household duties, changing diapers, and also teaching them school subjects—subjects that I am not good at myself. Help!*

*A*nswer: Consider home school and being at home from a different perspective. If you think of it as "confinement" that's all it will soon become. This is a season where you will find yourself saying "no" to the many things that appeal to you—activities, opportunities, and the like. You are saying "yes" to your family for now, in terms of the time, energy, and availability to be there for them. Bask in the moment, and ask the Lord to help you be content in this season, because it really is rushing by.

Question: *How do I teach our child to work for what he wants, and to be responsible and not spoiled? We grew up poor, and had great lessons to teach us discipline and honor and hard work.*

Answer: Begin modeling positive character traits for your child. It is easier to teach our children and develop positive character traits when they see we believe it ourselves.

CPSIA information can be obtained at www.ICGtesting.com
Printed in the USA
BVOW08s1601150614

356306BV00002B/4/P